Insects and Spiders
of the World

VOLUME 4
ENDANGERED SPECIES – GYPSY MOTH

Marshall Cavendish
New York • London • Toronto • Sydney

Marshall Cavendish
99 White Plains Road
Tarrytown, New York 10591

Website: www.marshallcavendish.com

Library of Congress Cataloging-in-Publication Data
Insects and spiders of the world.
    p.   cm.
    Contents: v. 1. Africanized bee–Bee fly — v. 2. Beetle–Carpet beetle — v. 3. Carrion beetle–Earwig — v. 4. Endangered species–Gyspy moth v. 5. Harvester ant–Leaf-cutting ant — v. 6. Locomotion–Orb-web spider — v. 7. Owlet moth–Scorpion — v. 8. Scorpion fly–Stinkbug — v. 9. Stone fly–Velvet worm — v. 10. Wandering spider–Zorapteran — v. 11. Index.
    ISBN 0-7614-7334-3 (set) — ISBN 0-7614-7335-1 (v. 1) — ISBN 0-7614-7336-X (v. 2) — ISBN 0-7614-7337-8 (v. 3) — ISBN 0-7614-7338-6 (v. 4) — ISBN 0-7614-7339-4 (v. 5) — ISBN 0-7614-7340-8 (v. 6) — ISBN 0-7614-7341-6 (v. 7) — ISBN 0-7614-7342-4 (v. 8) — ISBN 0-7614-7343-2 (v. 9) — ISBN 0-7614-7344-0 (v. 10) — ISBN 0-7614-7345-9 (v. 11)
    1. Insects. 2. Spiders.   I. Marshall Cavendish Corporation.

QL463 .I732 2003
595.7—dc21

                                                            2001028882

ISBN 0-7614-7334-3 (set)
ISBN 0-7614-7338-6 (volume 4)

Printed in Hong Kong

06 05 04 03 02   6 5 4 3 2 1

Brown Partworks Limited
Project Editor: Tom Jackson
Subeditor: Jim Martin
Managing Editor: Bridget Giles
Design: Graham Curd for WDA
Picture Researcher: Helen Simm
Illustrations: Wildlife Art Limited
Graphics: Darren Awuah, Dax Fullbrook, Mark Walker
Indexer: Kay Ollerenshaw

Marshall Cavendish
Editor: Joyce Tavolacci
Editorial Director: Paul Bernabeo

WRITERS
Dr. Robert S. Anderson
Richard Beatty
Dr. Stuart Church
Trevor Day
Dr. Arthur V. Evans
Amanda J. Harman
Dr. Rob Houston
Anne K. Jamieson
Becca Law
Professor Steve Marshall
Jamie McDonald
Ben Morgan
Dr. Kieren Pitts
Rebecca Saunders
Dr. Joseph L. Thorley
Dr. Gavin Wilson

COVER: Common blue butterfly **(Bruce Coleman Collection)**
TITLE PAGE: Long-horned beetle **(Bruce Coleman Collection)**

PICTURE CREDITS
Agricultural Research Service, USDA: Scott Bauer 200, 201, 202b, 206, 214, 233b, Christine Bennet 229b, Jack Dykinga 233t; **Art Explosion**: 207t, 207b, 208t, 208b, 226, 241b, 243; **Artville**: Burke & Triolo 202b; **Bruce Coleman Collection**: M.P. L. Fogden 237, 241t, Kim Taylor 231, Petr Zabransky 248, 251t; **David Clarke**: 236; **Corbis**: Jim Zuckerman 224t; **Educational Images Ltd**: 224b, 227b, Charles R. Belinky 246t, Ron West 239t, 247b; **Dr. A. V. Evans**: 217, 249; **Image Bank**: Image Makers / Burder 220; **NHPA**: Anthony Bannister 210, 225, G. I. Bernard 203, N. A. Callow 229t, N. R. Coulton 244, Stephen Dalton 227b, 247t, Robert Erwin 240, Image Quest 3-D 246b, Stephen Krasemann 212, Pavel German 234, Dr. Ivan Polunin 216, John Shaw 253t, Roger Tidman 197, Werner Zepf 253b; **Steve Marshall**: 199b, 213, 254; **Oxford Scientific Films**: John Brown 199t, Scott Camazine 215, Tina Catvaho 222, J. A. L. Cooke 205, Phil Devries 230, Harold Taylor 251b; **Papilio Photographic**: 196, 218; **Still Pictures**: Mark Edwards 198; **University of Florida**: Entomology Department 239b

CONTENTS

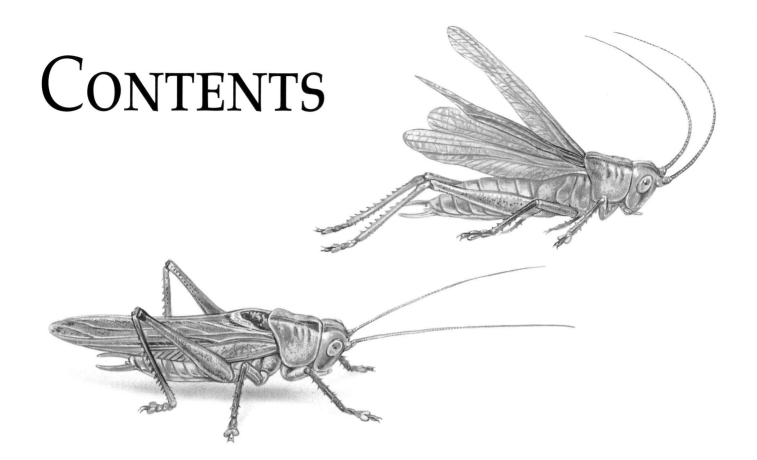

ENDANGERED SPECIES

Scientists do not know how many insect and spider species are threatened with extinction. It is likely that many thousands of species are disappearing with their habitats.

The first insects appeared more than 400 million years ago. By around 250 million years ago, insects had already become by far the most successful group of animals on Earth, with several million species and countless billions of individual insects.

However, just like many larger, more familiar animals, insect species are being wiped out by the impact of modern human activities on a range of habitats around the world.

Although we are not as numerous as insects, humans are a successful species in their own right. Two thousand years ago, the human population of the world was only 150 million, three-fifths of today's U.S. population. By the year 1700, the number of humans had risen to 600 million. By 2020,

▼ *A Rajah Brooke's bird-wing butterfly at rest. Bird-wing butterflies are often large and brightly colored, and some are very rare because they have been taken from the wild by collectors.*

DISTRIBUTION

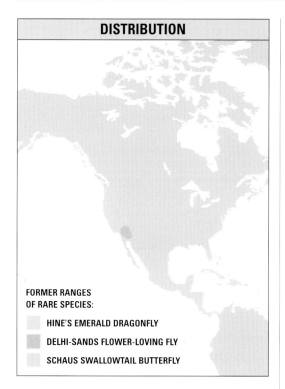

FORMER RANGES
OF RARE SPECIES:

HINE'S EMERALD DRAGONFLY

DELHI-SANDS FLOWER-LOVING FLY

SCHAUS SWALLOWTAIL BUTTERFLY

the human population will be well above 8 billion. It will have increased 13-fold in just 300 years. All of these people require places to live and produce food, and in doing so have had a dramatic effect on nature.

Upsetting the balance

From the point of view of many plants and animals, including insects, humans are the dominant pest species in the world. Human activities, such as clearing land for agriculture and cities, damming rivers for irrigation and electricity production, pumping pollution into the air and water, and burying trash in the ground have changed many of Earth's natural habitats completely, sometimes permanently.

Natural habitats are very complex, containing delicate webs of life that involve many types of plants, animals, fungi, and microorganisms, such as bacteria. Every species is linked with others, whether they are prey, predator, or competitor. Many species have closer relationships, or mutualisms, where one species relies on another for food or protection from enemies. When humans alter a habitat, by burning the trees or

polluting the water, at least some of the organisms that live in the area find it harder to survive. If all the members of a species die, that species becomes extinct, and other species that once had a relationship with it suffer. Plants and animals with small populations are liable to become extinct if nothing is done to protect them. They are called endangered or threatened species.

Unnatural enemies

Some species of insects are not just threatened by habitat destruction. Instead, species are being endangered as a result of trade—another human activity. When people move goods, such as wood, fruit, or fabric, around the world, they may also be transporting insects in their cargo. Many hundreds of species have been introduced to new continents in this way. Some of these species, such as fire ants and Africanized bees, spread across the land, killing off many of the area's natural inhabitants. The introduced species do this by directly preying on native species or by outcompeting them for food.

KEY FACTS

Name
Hine's emerald dragonfly (*Somatochlora hineana*)

Distinctive features
Brown and metallic green thorax; amber wings

Range
Once lived in wetlands south of the Great Lakes

▼ *A great raft spider walks across the surface of a wetland. This species of nursery-web spider lives in just a few European wetlands.*

Bird-wing butterflies

Bird-wing butterflies are the the largest butterflies in the world with wingspans of up to 11 inches (28 cm). They are easily recognized by their large size and the patterns on their wings, which are typically green, orange, and black. Bird-wings are classified as swallowtail butterflies, but they lack the characteristic tail-like extensions on the hind wings that are found on their more common relatives. Bird-wings live in the forests of Asia, New Guinea, parts of northern Australia, and on many Indonesian islands.

Some species of bird-wing butterflies, such as *Ornithoptera priamus* (of which there are several subspecies), are common, but others such as the world's largest, the Queen Alexandra's bird-wing, which lays the largest eggs of any insect, and *O. chimaera* are very rare and protected by international law. The reason for the decline of many species is the destruction of their forest habitat. The larvae of many species feed only on passion flowers found only in these tropical forests.

Some breeders are allowed to sell bird-wing butterflies to collectors. To satisfy the demand for these butterflies, many species are grown on farms in Papua New Guinea. This farming industry employs about 500 people throughout the country. Farming the insects for sale ensures that wild populations are left alone by collectors. However, it is still illegal to possess the rarest species.

KEY FACTS

Name
Schaus swallowtail (*Papilio aristodemus ponceanus*)

Distinctive features
Dark-brown wings with yellow markings

Range
Once lived from Miami to the Florida Keys. Now only lives in the upper Keys.

Image problems

When people are asked to name an endangered animal, they may say tiger, gorilla, or panda. However, it is very unlikely that anyone will list an insect or spider among those animals that are in need of saving from extinction. There are many reasons for this. One is the fact that several insect species have done very well living alongside humans. Species of flies, grasshoppers, and cockroaches, among many others, are commonly seen by people and are in need of no protection. In many cases, people try to kill as many of these insects as possible. In addition, many people are frightened of insects and hate spiders even more. These attitudes toward insects and spiders do not help efforts to protect threatened species.

However, by far the biggest problem facing conservationists is their own ignorance of which species of insects are endangered. Even if they do know that a species needs to be protected, the scientists may not understand why a population is in decline and therefore may not be able to protect it properly.

Experts estimate that more than half the animals on Earth are insects. However, entomologists have yet to record most of these insect species. Many conservationists claim that at least one species becomes extinct every day. It is probable that the real figure is higher, with many hundreds of species, most of them insects, being lost each year. It is very important to protect rare species; their disappearance affects other species and the habitat in general.

▶ *Insecticides are sprayed onto tea plants to keep the crops safe from pests. Insecticides will generally kill all the insects in an area, including endangered ones.*

◀ *A rain forest in Columbia. Rain forests are home to many rare insect species. The best way to protect them is to protect the forest itself.*

SEE ALSO

- *Arachnology*
- *Biological control*
- *Entomology*
- *Insect evolution*
- *Insecticide*

Keeping track

As a way of keeping track of species that are dropping in numbers, the World Conservation Union (IUCN) publishes a list of species at risk, called the Red List. Many countries, including the United States, use the list as a guide to which species require protection by law.

At present, most species protected by such laws are animals such as mammals, birds, reptiles, amphibians, mollusks, and fish, and many plants are also listed. Just a few insects are included in the listings, not because there are few endangered insects, but because scientists do not know enough to decide which ones are endangered.

Rare species

Scientists do know of some insects that are close to extinction. These include the brightly colored bird-wing butterflies of Southeast Asia and Australia, many other butterflies throughout the world, and a handful of dragonfly, beetle, bug, and fly species. These insects are now protected by law.

Species that are endangered in the United States include the American burying beetle, Schaus swallowtail butterfly (as well as 17 other butterflies), Hine's emerald dragonfly, Delhi-sands flower-loving fly, red-tailed prairie leafhopper, and phlox moth. The rarity of these species has been recognized, and their remaining habitats are now part of protected parks and reserves.

▼ *An American burying beetle. These insects are very rare, but scientists do not understand why.*

ENTOMOLOGY

Insects are often very important to people in many ways. Entomologists are scientists who study insects and their relationships with humans, other animals, and plants.

Insects live almost everywhere throughout the world and make up more than half of all living things on Earth. They play an important role in the natural world and our daily lives.

Many species are destructive pests, yet many others are beneficial to humans. Pests can damage garden plants and commercial crops, while others eat stored products. Some insects give a nasty bite or sting and can be carriers of dangerous diseases that affect domestic animals or human populations.

The importance of insects

Insects are essential to the balance of nature. They provide food for an enormous range of other animals. Parasitic wasps and flies control fast-growing populations of insects such as moths and bugs. Similarly, predatory larvae of insects such as lacewings and ladybugs keep the population of plant feeders, such as aphids, from growing too large. Decomposers and scavengers remove animal carcasses and dung and help recycle nutrients.

▼ *Entomologists use smoke and a modified vacuum cleaner to collect honeybees.*

In some parts of the world, insects are an important part of the diet of many people. They are also pollinators of many plants, including most orchard trees and many vegetables and field crops. Some species provide products of great economic importance such as honey, silk, and plasticlike shellac resins. Entomologists use many types of insects in biological control programs designed to minimize the damaging effects of pest species.

Insects in the laboratory

Insects are often used as the basis of scientific research in many different fields, from molecular biology to how body systems work to ecological relationships. The fruit fly *Drosophila* has been the main experimental organism used in genetics (study of inherited traits) research for many years.

By studying insects, entomologists add to our understanding of nature and to the improvement of our food, health, and standard of living. In the United States, losses caused by insects have been estimated at $3.5 billion each year; however, their beneficial role as pollinators alone is thought to be worth about $4.5 billion each year.

The history of entomology

Entomology has a long history, dating from at least 3000 B.C.E. when sacred scarab beetles were worshiped by the ancient Egyptians. There are also records that the Chinese used silkworms for the production of silk as early as 2700 B.C.E. Later, the Greeks revered the bee, which represented Artemis, goddess of fertility.

While the Greek philosopher Aristotle (384–322 B.C.E.) was the first to name many common insects, it was not until the invention of the microscope in the 17th century that entomology became a serious subject. Perhaps the most significant advance was the development of a system of scientific names for all living things by Carolus Linnaeus (1707–1778) in 1758. The Linnaean system provided

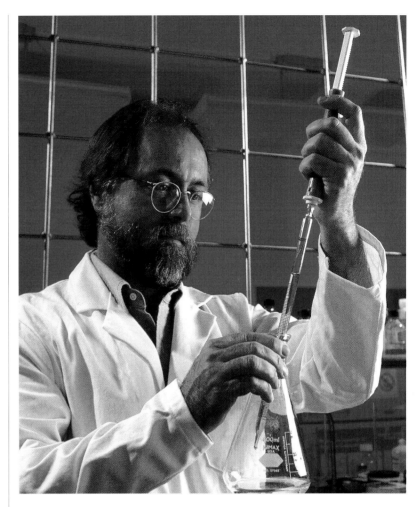

a means of organizing all sorts of information about the natural world in a simple and easy to understand way. The first publication on the subject was produced by British naturalist John Curtis. He published the final volume of *British Entomology* in 1839, which led to the study of insects becoming a distinct scientific field for the first time.

Inside entomology

Entomologists can have many different specializations. Some work at museums or universities and study insects to understand their classification, biology, ecology, and relationships to one another. Other entomologists seek ways to control insects. These scientists are concerned with the protection of crops and other foodstuffs from attack by insect pests. Many of them work on developing insecticides or new ways to use biological control agents against

▲ *This entomologist is studying the genetics of the honeybee.*

pest species. Medical entomologists study the relationships between insects and diseases. Many deadly human diseases, such as malaria, sleeping sickness, and encephalitis, are carried by insects. Millions of people die each year from these illnesses. The insects carry the tiny organisms responsible for these diseases and pass them on when they drink people's blood or contaminate their food with dirt and feces.

Environmental indicators

Another area of research involves using insects to measure the effects of pollution on the environment. For example, caddis fly larvae are generally found only in clear, unpolluted water, while rat-tailed maggots (a type of hover fly larva) flourish in water that has been polluted and is low in oxygen.

Insect remains can be used to tell what the climate was like long ago. Under the right conditions, the wing cases of beetles can remain in the soil for thousands of years. When archaeologists find beetle remains among human artifacts and identify the species, they can then assume that the local climate was once like that of the species' current range.

SEE ALSO

- *Arachnology*
- *Biological control*
- *Blowfly*
- *Carpet beetle*
- *Carrion beetle*
- *Honeybee*
- *Insecticide*
- *Pest*

▶ *These termites are feeding on a red dye. This will allow entomologists to track them as they forage.*

▼ *Many entomologists collect and pin insects like this so they can study them under a microscope.*

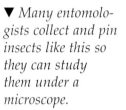

Entomological crime fighters

Insects often have an important role in police work. Blowflies, flesh flies, and many species of beetles lay their eggs on dead bodies, often at specific times after death. By identifying the species, the developmental stage the larvae have reached, and the temperature of the surroundings, entomologists can estimate the time of death. This is often of crucial importance in a murder investigation. The use of insects in police work is called forensic entomology

Forensic entomologists help solve many other crimes. For example, by identifying the pest insects present in a smuggled shipment, police officers can find out the probable country of origin.

Insect societies

Many professional and amateur societies are dedicated to the study of insects. The Young Entomologists Society of the United States aids the study of insects by young people.

FALSE SCORPION

These tiny relatives of spiders look a little like scorpions.
They have pincerlike claws on their forelimbs like true
scorpions, but false scorpions do not have stingers.

False scorpions, or pseudoscorpions, are arachnids that resemble scorpions but are much smaller and lack the long abdomen and stinger. Most of the 2,000 or so species live in the tropics. False scorpions generally live beneath stones, in moss or leaf litter, under bark, or in animal nests. Some live in caves, while a few species are sometimes found inside buildings. Others live on the seashore, rummaging between the tide lines for food. Some species hitch rides on the backs of beetles.

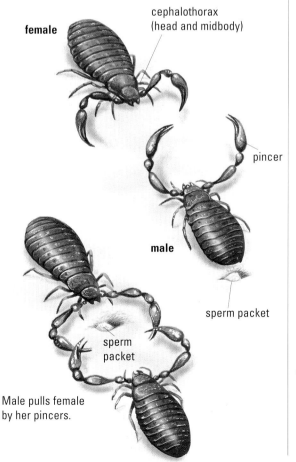

female

cephalothorax
(head and midbody)

pincer

male

sperm packet

sperm
packet

Male pulls female
by her pincers.

▲ *This false
scorpion lives in
the dead wood of
a fallen tree. False
scorpions like this
one also live
in birds' and
mammals' nests.*

◄ *False scorpions
mating. The male
drops a packet of
sperm on the
ground and waves
his pincers. A
female approaches
and he pulls her
over the packet. The
sperm enters her
abdomen and fertil-
izes the eggs.*

Real poison

False scorpions can move backward as easily as they move forward. They use their large pincerlike claws for grasping small animal prey, such as aphids and worms. False scorpions produce venom that paralyzes their prey, but they do not pose any danger to humans. They also manufacture silk to build retreats for hibernation, molting, and laying eggs.

Most false scorpions range in size from 0.2 to 0.3 inches (4 to 8 mm). Many species have up to four simple eyes, while others are totally blind. Because their eyesight is weak at best, false scorpions rely on their sense of touch to find food and detect danger. Their large, pincerlike claws are extremely sensitive to touch. Each claw is equipped with a fixed and movable finger, one or both of which have poison glands. A false

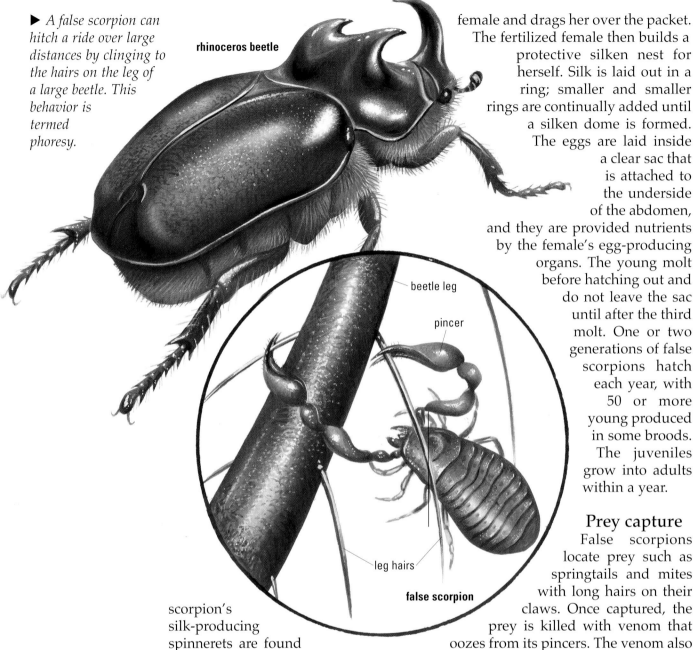

▶ *A false scorpion can hitch a ride over large distances by clinging to the hairs on the leg of a large beetle. This behavior is termed phoresy.*

rhinoceros beetle

beetle leg

pincer

leg hairs

false scorpion

female and drags her over the packet. The fertilized female then builds a protective silken nest for herself. Silk is laid out in a ring; smaller and smaller rings are continually added until a silken dome is formed. The eggs are laid inside a clear sac that is attached to the underside of the abdomen, and they are provided nutrients by the female's egg-producing organs. The young molt before hatching out and do not leave the sac until after the third molt. One or two generations of false scorpions hatch each year, with 50 or more young produced in some broods. The juveniles grow into adults within a year.

Prey capture

False scorpions locate prey such as springtails and mites with long hairs on their claws. Once captured, the prey is killed with venom that oozes from its pincers. The venom also digests the prey's body tissues, turning them into liquid, which is sucked up by the false scorpion.

Because they are small and wingless, false scorpions find traveling over long distances difficult. Long-horned and scarab beetles unwittingly carry these tiny hitchhikers on their legs and under their wings. One species climbs aboard the Central American harlequin beetle to find new tree stumps for feeding and laying eggs. When the beetle lands on a log, the false scorpion slides off to explore its new home.

scorpion's silk-producing spinnerets are found on its sharp, fanglike mouthparts. A false scorpion breathes through two pairs of spiracles (air holes) located beneath its abdomen.

Life cycle

The courtship of false scorpions varies among different species. False scorpion males generally deposit a single sperm packet on the ground to be picked up by the female. Females locate the packet by touch and smell, or are guided to it by a silk line left by the male. In some species, the male grasps the claws of the

SEE ALSO

• *Arthropod*
• *Harvestman*
• *Scorpion*
• *Sun spider*
• *Symbiosis*
• *Tick and mite*
• *Whip scorpion*

FEEDING

Insects and spiders feed in an amazing number of different ways and on a wide range of foods—plants and animals, the living and the dead. Some even feed on humans.

About half of all insect species feed on living plants. The parts of plants that insects eat include the leaves, stalks, pollen, nectar, sap, fruit, seeds, and roots. Many insects and all spiders are meat eaters, feeding on other insects or other invertebrates, such as worms and slugs. Some other insects feed on decaying material, such as wood, feces, and dead animals. For just about any possible source of food on land, there is an insect species that makes use of it. Ecologically, insects are very important, because in the process of breaking down decaying material they release essential nutrients back into the environment.

Avoiding competition

It is common for the adult and larval forms of some insect species to feed in different ways and on different foods. For example, in most species of butterfly, the caterpillars eat leaves, while the adults feed on nectar. So, adults and young are not in competition with each other for the same food source.

Some insects, such as the American cockroach and many other pest species, are highly adaptable and will eat almost anything they can find. Other species are more specialized and are restricted to just one food source. For example, the caterpillar of the monarch butterfly will feed only on the leaves of milkweed plants, while bat flies feed exclusively on the blood of bats.

Insect mouthparts

The mouthparts of an insect were once limbs that have evolved into feeding organs. Grasshoppers and cockroaches have the most basic organization of

◀ A queen leaf-cutting ant and some workers feed on fungus grown on decaying leaves inside an ants' nest.

mouthparts; other insects have evolved adaptations that make their jaws better suited to their particular feeding habits.

Insect mouthparts consist of four main elements. The mandibles are the parts most similar to jaws, and they are often used by the insect to cut up food. Predatory insects, such as praying mantises, have large, strong mandibles that close like pincers from the sides of the mouth. Some sucking insects, such as mosquitoes, have long, needle-like mandibles, which form a kind of hypodermic syringe for drawing blood from the insects' victims.

Feeding inside a host

Insects from several groups spend part of their lives as parasites, living inside and feeding on the body of the host. These include the larvae of parasitic wasps, a large group that attacks a variety of other inverte-brates, including caterpillars, bugs, and spiders. The victim is paralyzed before being buried in a chamber in the soil, and the wasp lays an egg inside the animal. After hatching, the larva feeds on the still-living but paralyzed host, eating it from the inside out.

Ants have a wide range of different mouthparts, even within the same species. A number of insect groups, such as the butterflies, have no mandibles.

Sucking tubes and sponges

Another element of the mouthparts are the maxillae, or secondary jaws. In primitive insects, the maxillae are used to hold food, but they have a range of uses in other groups. In butterflies, for example, the maxillae are joined together by an arrangement of hooks and loops. This forms a long, flexible tube (called a proboscis) that is used to draw nectar from flowers.

Some moths feed on blood, and they have sharp spines at the end of the proboscis. These spines allow them to rasp away at their victim's skin before they suck up the blood. In fleas, the maxillae form two long cutting blades, used to break the skin of the host.

Another mouthpart is the labium, or lower lip. Like the maxillae, this takes a wide variety of forms. In the housefly the labium is like a sponge that can be spread out over the surface of food.

▲ *A 14-spot ladybug feeds on a pea aphid. Both adult and larval ladybugs feed on aphids. They do not compete, though, since they prey on different types of aphids and bugs.*

KEY WORDS

Mandibles
The insect equiv-alent of jaws; used for cutting and holding food items

Maxillae
Secondary jaws used to hold food and at times to cut; can also form a proboscis

Labrum & labium
Upper and lower lips

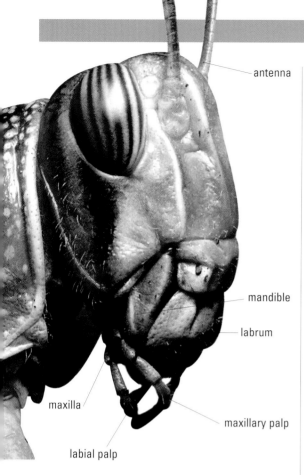

antenna

mandible

labrum

maxilla

maxillary palp

labial palp

Digesting food

Digestion in insects begins with saliva, which flows along a tonguelike organ on the floor of the mouth called the hypopharynx. Many insects and spiders digest their prey outside the body. The saliva is poured or injected onto food, dissolving the solid material. The insect then sucks up the juices. Insects that feed on blood have saliva that contains anticoagulants. These proteins help keep blood running freely by preventing clotting. Some bugs, such as aphids and scale insects, have saliva that solidifies to form a sheath around the mouthparts, making them stiff enough to pierce plant stems and suck out the sap.

The insect gut

After swallowing, food enters the gut, which is divided into three regions separated by muscular valves. Each of the three gut regions has a particular function. The foregut includes the salivary glands and is involved in the storage and grinding of food. The midgut secretes digestive juices and absorbs nutrients from the food, while the hindgut absorbs water and salts from the digested material and forms the feces (droppings). The overall structure of an insect's gut depends on the

◀ *A grasshopper's mandibles open and close like shears to cut up plants. The maxillae are used to hold food and sometimes have sharp attachments for cutting. The labium is mainly a sensory organ—palps on both the labium and maxillae taste the food. The labrum guides food into the mouth.*

▼ *A moth keeps its proboscis coiled under its head. This tubelike mouthpart uncoils for feeding, during which it sucks up liquids such as nectar.*

Enzymes are secreted from many small tubes in the labium; these chemicals begin to digest the food by liquefying it. The resulting mush is then sucked up by the fly's proboscis. In dragonfly nymphs, the labium is enlarged into a long, grasping arm with sharp hooks at the end (the mask). This folds under the head at rest but can be extended very quickly to grab prey.

Insect mouthparts are completed by the palps, which are the insect equivalent of taste buds. These often bulblike organs contain many cells sensitive to both taste and texture, and they are used to examine food before it is eaten.

Insects without mouthparts

A number of insects, such as mayflies and some species of butterflies, have no mouthparts as adults. They feed only as larvae, and the adults only live long enough to reproduce. Other parts of the body may also be adapted to help the insect feed. For example, many predatory insects, such as the water scorpion and the praying mantis, have strong front legs with claws to grasp their prey.

◀ *A bug feeds on a flower head. Among the most specialized of all liquid feeders, bugs have tubelike mouthparts for sucking up liquids.*

KEY WORDS

Chelicerae
Arachnid mouthparts to which the fangs are attached

Crop
Front part of the gut used for food storage

Gut microorganism
Tiny animal living inside the insect gut, where it helps digest compounds such as cellulose

Rostrum
Bug mouthparts containing a stylet (fused maxillae and mandibles) sheathed by a tubelike labium

Saliva
Secretions containing enzymes that begin to digest food

type of food the insect eats. Insects that feed on low-nutrient liquids have long, narrow guts that keep food inside the gut for longer so there is more time for the digestion and absorption of nutrients. By contrast, insects feeding on solid food often have a wide, short, straight gut, with strong muscles. Many species also have a grinding organ, called the gizzard, which helps break up tough bits of food.

Plant eaters need to eat more than meat eaters, because their food is less nutritious. However, they are able to feed more or less all the time, because plant food is constantly available. Prey-hunting insects have to be more ready to take every opportunity to eat when food is available. For this reason, many meat-eating insects have a gut with a large storage area, or crop, allowing them to go some time without feeding.

Keeping microorganisms out

The exoskeleton of the insect extends into both the foregut and hindgut, protecting the insect from invasion by microorganisms. The midgut needs to absorb nutrients, so it cannot have such a continuous lining, but it does secrete a protective membrane over the food as it passes through. This is made of chitin, the same material that makes up the insect's outer covering. The membrane has a tiny hole in it, however, providing a degree of protection while still allowing nutrients to be released. Insects that feed on wood, such as termites and wood cockroaches, have microorganisms in the hindgut that enable them to digest tough plant fibers.

Filter-feeding

Some aquatic insect larvae, such as mosquitoes, are filter feeders. These larvae have brushlike mouthparts made up of bristles, or setae, which trap fine food particles when water is sucked through them. Caddis fly larvae filter-feed in a different manner. They spin a silken net, which they sweep through the water or hold in the current. They then remove any food particles caught in the net with their mouthparts.

Feeding in spiders

All spiders are predators. They have mouthparts called chelicerae, which have sharp fangs with poison glands at the base. The fangs pierce the skin of the

▶ *This spider has caught a fly. The yellow and black coloration of the fly suggests that it contains distasteful chemicals or poisons. Spiders are generally tolerant of these chemicals and will eat many insects that are avoided by birds and other more choosy predators.*

HOW SPIDERS FEED

1) A spider bites its prey, injecting paralyzing venom through its fangs at the ends of the chelicerae. Many species wrap their prey in silk before biting.

2) The spider vomits up (regurgitates) fluids from its gut onto its prey. The fluids contain enzymes that begin the process of digesting the prey.

abdomen

Channel for poison inside chelicera. The fang is buried inside the prey.

side view

eye

pharynx

chelicera

throat

labium (lip)

insect prey, with hard outer covering (exoskeleton)

Food is pumped into the stomach by the pharynx.

3) After a few seconds, the spider starts to suck the liquid food up through its mouth, which lies between the chelicerae. Solid particles are filtered out. Further digestion and absorption of nutrients take place in the midgut. Some spiders have spikelike teeth on the tips of the chelicera at the base of each fang. These spiders rip their prey into shreds as they eat; spiders that have no cheliceral teeth suck the insides of their prey out, leaving the empty exoskeleton virtually intact.

mouth

chelicera

view from above

poison channel

chelicera

Plant defenses against bugs

All bugs have sucking mouthparts, and many bugs suck sap from the leaves and stems of plants. However, sap is a relatively poor food source, low in nitrogen-containing nutrients. The bugs also have to contend with a range of plant defenses.

Many plants have thick, waxy cuticles and hairs that might ensnare small bugs. Some produce toxins, such as hydrogen cyanide, which is present in the sap; others release compounds that are harmless until acted on by digestive secretions, which alter them into very poisonous chemicals. A few plants have a more subtle antibug defense—they manufacture imitation hormones, which interfere with the insect's growth and molting cycle.

The bugs fight back by using complex enzyme systems to break the compounds down. Also, some bugs are not affected by the poisons and find food by detecting them.

victim, and then the fangs inject venom that either paralyzes or kills the prey. Finally, the spider pours digestive juices into the wound to dissolve the soft inner parts into a soup and then sucks the fluid out, leaving behind nothing but a dry husk.

Although most spiders feed on insects, larger species such as tarantulas sometimes eat vertebrates such as frogs, snakes, and birds. Some prefer to feed on vertebrates, even if large insect prey is available. Other arthropods, such as scorpions and centipedes, also use venom to subdue their struggling prey.

▲ *A spider eats a fly. Spiders differ in the position of the fangs at the tips of their chelicerae. In some, the fangs swing out from the chelicerae and stab down into prey. Other spiders, such as the one shown here, swing their chelicerae out to the side and have fangs that point inward.*

SEE ALSO

- *Anatomy and physiology*
- *Senses*

FIG WASP

Fig wasps and fig plants could not exist without each other. The plants rely on the wasps for pollination, and the wasps can breed only inside a fig. The tiny wasps have been introduced around the world by fig growers.

Figs are not true fruits; they are hollow structures with flowers on the inside. In some species, male and female flowers are found inside each fig; these species are called monoecious. Other figs have separate male and female trees and are termed dioecious.

Amazing life cycles

Each species of fig wasp is adapted to live in tandem with one of the 750 species of figs. Those wasps suited to monoecious figs have one of the most incredible life cycles of any insect. The larvae hatch inside the ovaries of the fig and feed on the seeds before pupating. Around three months after hatching, the adult males chew their way out of the ovary. The males are eyeless and wingless. Still inside the fig, they crawl to a flower that contains a female wasp and chew a hole in the wall before mating with the female inside. The males mate with every female inside the fig. They have one more important role to perform before dying—the males work together to chew a circular tunnel through the tough skin of the fig.

Inside the fig, carbon dioxide levels are usually very high, several times higher than in the air outside. When the males break through the skin, the amount of this gas inside the fig drops, stirring the females into

action. They escape from the ovaries through the holes chewed by the males. At the same time, the male flowers inside the fig begin to produce pollen.

The females collect pollen from the flowers, packing it into a pair of "baskets" on their bodies. They emerge from the tunnel cut by the males and look for receptive figs. The figs guide the wasps by releasing chemicals into the air. The female enters the fig through a tiny hole at the top, called an ostiole. This is very small, and some wasps have barbs on their legs and mouthparts to help haul themselves through. Nonetheless, the

▲ *Some fig wasps cheat the system. They have very long ovipositors, which they use to lay eggs inside the longer-styled ovaries without pollinating the flowers beforehand.*

▶ *The life cycle of a fig wasp, inside a monoecious species of fig.*

1) A female wasp enters the fig through the ostiole.

ostiole

2) The female lays eggs in short-styled flowers.

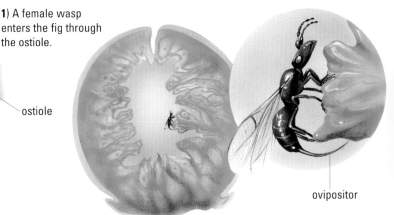

ovipositor

DISTRIBUTION

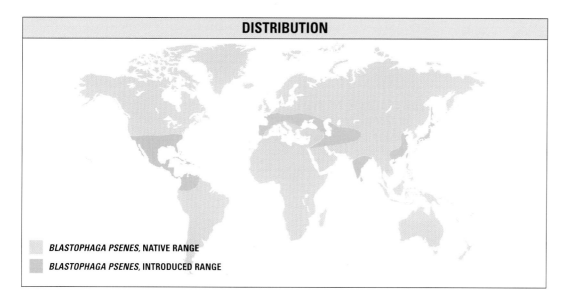

■ *BLASTOPHAGA PSENES*, NATIVE RANGE

■ *BLASTOPHAGA PSENES*, INTRODUCED RANGE

KEY FACTS

Name
Blastophaga psenes (no common name)

Distinctive features
Female is shiny black and winged, and has a thread-like ovipositor; male is yellow and wingless with a tapering abdomen

Breeding
Female lays eggs inside figs, which she pollinates in order to feed her larvae

Size
Up to 0.08 inches (2 mm) long

SEE ALSO

- *Parasitic wasp*
- *Pollination*
- *Spider wasp*
- *Symbiosis*
- *Wasp*

squeeze is often so tight that the entering wasp loses her wings in the process. Most ostioles close after the fig wasp enters, keeping other insects out.

The female wasp actively pollinates the flowers with the pollen she has brought; this ensures that seeds will develop, allowing the larvae to feed. She lays one egg in each available fig ovary before dying, although in a couple of species, the females crawl back through the ostiole to lay eggs in another fig.

Wasps in dioecious figs do not use pollen baskets to purposefully pollinate the figs; pollination is accidental, but still vital for both the figs' and the wasps' ability to reproduce. Close beneficial relationships between two species such as these are called mutualisms.

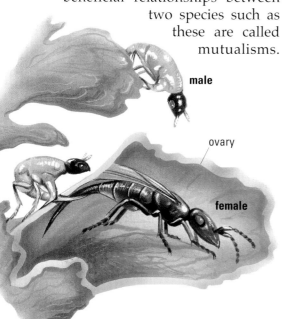

male

ovary

female

After pollination, the fig ripens and becomes attractive food for many animals, such as monkeys and fruit bats, that help disperse the seeds of the fig throughout the forest in their feces.

Phony fig wasps

Fig wasps are highly specific to their hosts. Each species of fig is pollinated by just one species of wasp (or very rarely, two). The opening of the fig flower inside the fruit is connected to the ovary via a short tube termed a style. Styles can be either short or long, but most fig wasps have short ovipositors (egg tubes) and can only lay eggs in short-styled flowers.

Long-styled flowers are left for seed production alone. However, some fig wasps cheat; they lay their eggs without doing any pollinating, sometimes using very long ovipositors to penetrate the fig walls. The larvae of these wasps may eat the fig seeds from long-styled flowers, which were out of reach of the genuine fig wasps, or they may even feed on the other fig wasp larvae.

3) After pupation, the males chew a tunnel into an ovary to mate with the female inside.

4) The males chew an exit tunnel in the wall of the fig.

5) The pregnant females emerge and head for another fig.

FIRE ANT

Fire ants are aggressive pests that compete fiercely with other ant species. They get their name from their burning sting, which feels as if a flame is being held against the skin.

At least 13 different species of ants have been given the common name "fire ant." These include the native U.S. fire ant, the black imported fire ant, the red imported fire ant, and another introduced species, the little fire ant.

The one thing all these insects have in common is the hot, burning sting with which they defend themselves. This weapon is mainly used against their prey or against rival ants, but these fierce little creatures will sting any animals, including people, that get in their way. The poison from fire ant stings hardly ever kills people, but it produces a red itchy patch on the skin. In stings made by the imported species of fire ants, this patch fills with pus within a few days and can easily become infected with bacteria.

Fire ants are most numerous and common in hot tropical areas. However, fire ant species are also found in many countries inside the cooler temperate

▼ *Inside a red imported fire ant colony. Worker ants can be seen tending to white eggs and pupae inside the nest's tunnels.*

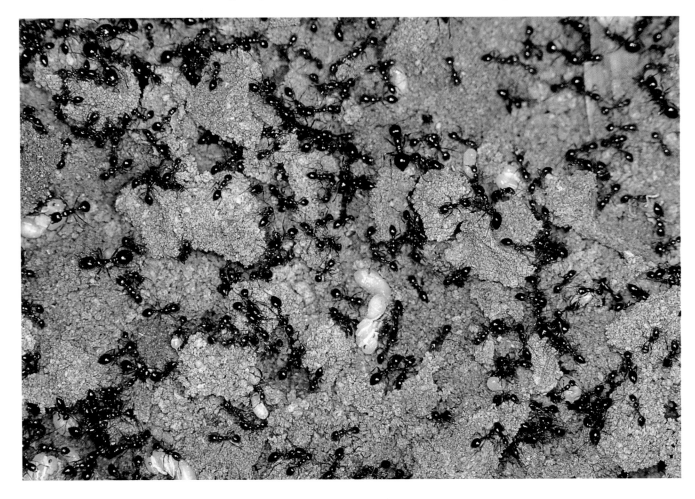

DISTRIBUTION

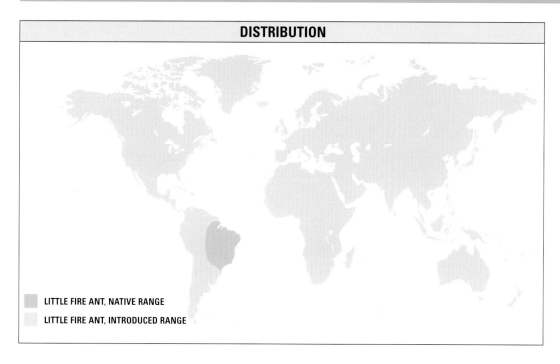

▪ LITTLE FIRE ANT, NATIVE RANGE
▫ LITTLE FIRE ANT, INTRODUCED RANGE

▼ *A man's leg covered in fire ant stings. A person will often get attacked by many fire ants at once because the insects live in large groups.*

zones (those parts of Earth between the tropics and the polar regions). Some of these species have been introduced accidentally by people settling in new parts of the world. In these places, the ants have often become serious pests because they have no natural predators to control their population.

Once they move into a new area, fire ants soon make their presence felt. Their colonies grow very rapidly, and the ants begin to crowd out other insects by taking their source of food or by killing them. The ants also eat their way through huge quantities of commercial crops, damage homes and equipment, and sting people and their livestock. Some animals—including dogs, cattle, tortoises, and elephants—have even been known to go blind after their eyes have been stung by fire ants.

Tramp ants

Some fire ants are also called tramp ants because they are often found in soil or food being transported on ships, or even in automobiles and on trains. Good examples of tramp species are the two imported fire ants, which get their name because they came into the southern United States from their natural home in South America by this method.

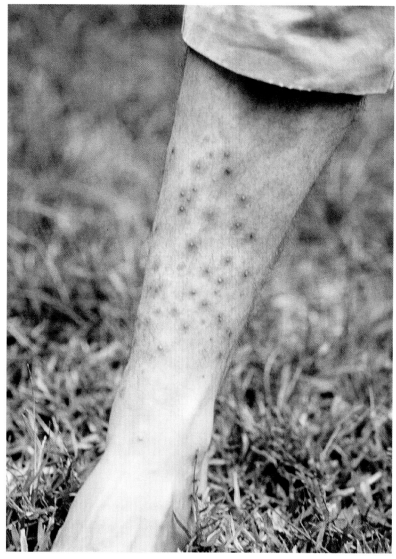

Taking aim at fire ants

In areas where they have been introduced, fire ant species have been causing many problems for farmers and their animals. Chemical pesticides are not very effective, and so scientists started looking for a natural enemy that could be used in a biological control program.

A suitable candidate was soon found. Tiny ant-decapitating flies lay their eggs inside the body of ants, including fire ants. The fly's wormlike larva hatches out and begins eating its way through the ant's body toward the head. The larva may eat so much of the ant's insides that its head falls off. The larva pupates inside the ant's head or body before emerging as an adult. Not only do they kill fire ants in large numbers, but just the presence of these flies in their nest appears to make the ants less aggressive.

▼ *Fire ants on the move. As well as giving painful stings, fire ants are also serious crop pests.*

The black imported fire ant arrived in the port of Mobile, Alabama, in 1918 and soon spread to Mississippi and southern Tennessee. Its close cousin, the red imported fire ant, is even more of a traveler. Since it arrived in Mobile in the 1930s, it has advanced throughout the southern states, and today it is abundant from South Carolina and Florida in the east across to Oklahoma and Texas. Today, red imported fire ants dominate all other species of ants in these states. The species is still moving northward and westward at a rate of about five miles a year, and sightings of the red imported fire ants have already been made in Kansas and California. So far, attempts to control the red imported ant have failed. Appropriately, the second word of this species' scientific name, *Solenopsis invicta*, means the "unconquered one."

The little fire ant is just as much of a tramp species as the imported fire ants. It has spread from the southern United States to the Caribbean island of Puerto Rico, the Galápagos, and the Solomons. It has even turned up in west Africa. Scientists fear that this species may one day reach Australia, where it would devastate that area's wildlife.

Red imported fire ant

Scientists know more about the red imported fire ant than they do about any other type of fire ant, and probably more than they know about any other ant species. It is such a hardy species that artificial nests, containing as many as 20,000 individual ants, can be kept in the laboratory very easily.

Like other ants, these creatures are social insects, and in the wild they live in large colonies. The only ant in a fire ant colony that can reproduce is the queen, which lays around 1,600 eggs each day. Most of these become wingless daughters called workers. Worker ants perform all the tasks that keep the colony running, such as looking after the eggs and young developing ants, cleaning the nest, foraging for food, and defending the colony from attack by other ants. Fire ants work together so efficiently that they are a powerful force, even though each ant is no bigger than 0.2 inches (4 mm) long.

Reproduction

Every year the queen also produces many thousands of winged sons and daughters. Unlike their worker sisters, these winged ants are able to breed. They fly out of the nest, usually in the spring and fall following heavy rains, and mate in the air with winged ants from other fire ant colonies. Female

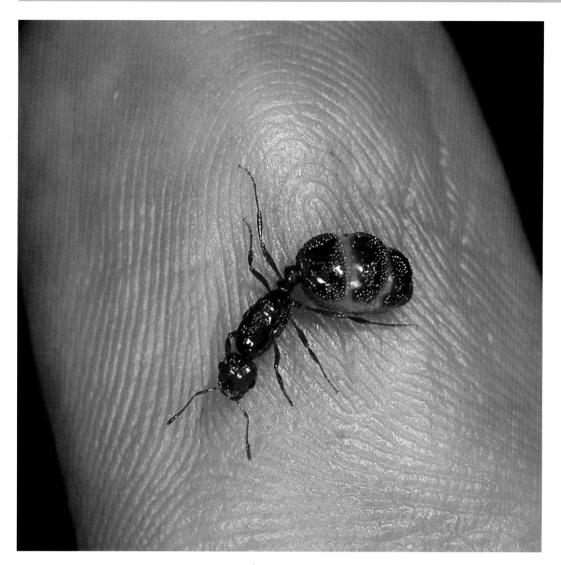

KEY FACTS

Name
Red imported fire ant (*Solenopsis invicta*)

Distinctive features
Reddish brown worker, black male, stinger at the end of the abdomen

Habitat
Soil in grasslands, meadows, and fields; nests are loose mounds with craters in surface for ventilation

Food
Eats both plants and animals especially seedlings and insects

Lifespan
Worker lives for 5 weeks, queen can live for 7 years

Size
0.2 inches (4 mm)

SEE ALSO

winged ants are large and red, while the males are black and have a smaller head. Once they have mated, the males die. The newly mated females land on the ground, shed their wings, and look for a patch of ground to dig into and begin a new colony as the queen ant.

Safely settled in a small chamber around 1 inch (25 to 30 mm) under the soil, the queen lays her first batch of between 10 and 15 eggs. These hatch out into young worker ants, which begin to feed and care for her once they have developed into adults. The queen continues to lay eggs for the rest of her life, which may last seven years.

On many occasions, a new colony of red imported fire ants starts off with two or more queens. In some colonies, the workers kill off the weaker or less fertile queens until only one is left. In other colonies, workers allow more than one queen to live in the same nest. A fully grown colony of these fire ants can have as many as half a million workers.

Little fire ants

Colonies of little fire ants are very similar to those of the red imported fire ants, except in the way they breed. This species does not have mating flights. Instead, the young wingless queens mate with their brothers inside the nest and take a group of workers to start a colony nearby. This type of colony reproduction in ants is known as budding, and it can result in a huge "supercolony" that expands farther and farther outward and contains many queens and their workers.

FIREFLY AND GLOWWORM

Glowing brightly after dark, fireflies are actually beetles. They communicate using flashes of light. The chemicals involved in their light production have important applications in medicine.

Fireflies or lightning bugs are neither flies nor bugs, but flat, soft-bodied beetles. There are about 2,000 species of fireflies around the world, mostly living in the tropics. Of the 140 species found in North America, most live in the eastern United States.

Fireflies are best known for the ability of some species to produce light to locate mates, to attract prey, and to discourage predators. Their light-producing organs are white or yellow and are located on the underside of the abdomen. Even the eggs, larvae, and pupae of some species glow in the dark. Night-active, light-producing species spend the day hiding beneath bark, in leaf litter, or resting on leaves. Fireflies with weak or no light-producing organs at all are active during the day and are often found on flowers. Male fireflies have large eyes with which they detect the dim light produced by the females.

The head of an adult firefly is partly or completely concealed by the thorax (midbody). Their wing cases usually cover their abdomens but are very small in the females of a few species.

▼ *The light-producing reaction used by fireflies is almost 100-percent efficient, and very little energy is wasted as heat.*

Glowworms

Some adult females look more like grubs (larvae) than beetles and are called glowworms. Many insects go through a pupal stage, when the larva changes into an adult. Glowworms retain many of their larval characteristics after pupation but become sexually mature. Unlike their larvae, adult glowworms have compound eyes.

Glowing in the dark

Bioluminescence (light production) in fireflies is used primarily to locate and identify mates. The color of the firefly's light varies between species from light green to orange and may be influenced by temperature and humidity. The light-producing organs are located beneath segments of the firefly's abdomen. These organs are supplied with air by many breathing tubes, or tracheae. By regulating the oxygen supply, fireflies can control the brightness and frequency of their flashes.

Light is produced by a series of chemical reactions. Adenosine triphosphate, shortened to ATP, is essential to all types of organisms and functions as an energy transporter. An enzyme called luciferinase joins ATP to molecules of a compound called luciferin. This gives energy to the luciferin, which then reacts with oxygen molecules carried to it by the tracheae. The reaction releases energy in the form of a spark of light.

Occurring at the same time, the sparks of thousands of cells in the light-producing organs combine to produce a flash of light clearly visible to the human eye.

Energy efficiency

Bioluminescence in fireflies is almost 100-percent efficient; almost all the energy that goes into the system is given off as light. A light bulb is not nearly as efficient, with 90 percent of the electrical energy lost as heat. The light organ of one firefly yields only one-hundred-thousandth of the heat produced by a candle flame of similar brightness.

Males fly at night, repeatedly flashing their signal until receiving an answer from a female perched on a rock or plant. The signals vary among species from rapid, rhythmic bursts to long, sustained flashes over a period of time. The number, speed, and duration of the male's signal, and the delay and length of the female response vary with each species. This interaction continues for five to ten exchanges until the insects finally meet. Female glowworms may glow continuously to attract males.

Emitting light together

Fireflies in tropical Asia band together on trees in vast numbers, flashing their lights at the same time to increase the

◄ *The females of some species become sexually mature while retaining the body of a larva. Here, three males are trying to mate with one such female.*

chances of attracting a mate. At first, the light emissions are not synchronized (in time) with each other, but each firefly gradually adjusts its flashing to match its neighbor's, until eventually the whole group flashes in tandem. Several firefly species may occupy the tree at the same time, each sending out their own unique signal. Synchronized flashing can be seen from miles away and often continues all night throughout the breeding season.

Deadly deception

After mating, the females of some species alter their flash pattern to attract males from different species of fireflies. They do so not to attract a mate, but an easy meal instead. Not only does this provide a source of food, but these females also gain important defensive chemicals from their victims, which the hunters are unable to produce themselves. These chemicals protect the fireflies from predators such as jumping spiders.

Females of at least 12 species of fireflies prey upon males of other species. Deception like this, where one animal dupes another before preying upon it, is called aggressive mimicry.

Flashing together in America

Recent research has shown that synchronized flashing in fireflies is not limited to Southeast Asia. Groups of Georgia coastal plain fireflies flash in tandem for a while, then change their rhythm, but synchronize again later. This is called intermittent synchrony and is unknown in other fireflies.

Eggs and young

Female fireflies dig holes in the ground into which they lay small clusters of eggs. Firefly larvae are tapered at both ends and flattened. Their bodies are composed of brightly marked plates. They have small, retractable heads equipped with simple eyes and armed with hollow mouthparts. They hunt for their food, which includes invertebrates such as millipedes, slugs, and small insects. The prey are paralyzed with enzymes that the fireflies pump through their mouthparts. The enzymes also digest the internal organs of the prey, which are then sucked out by the firefly.

Enemies and defense

Some fireflies have pungent odors and are known to be distasteful to monkeys, bats, and ducks. Bioluminescence in

◄ *This female firefly is replying to the flash signals from a nearby male. The female must provide the correct flash sequence in return and leave just the right amount of time before replying. If the response is not perfect, the male will fly away.*

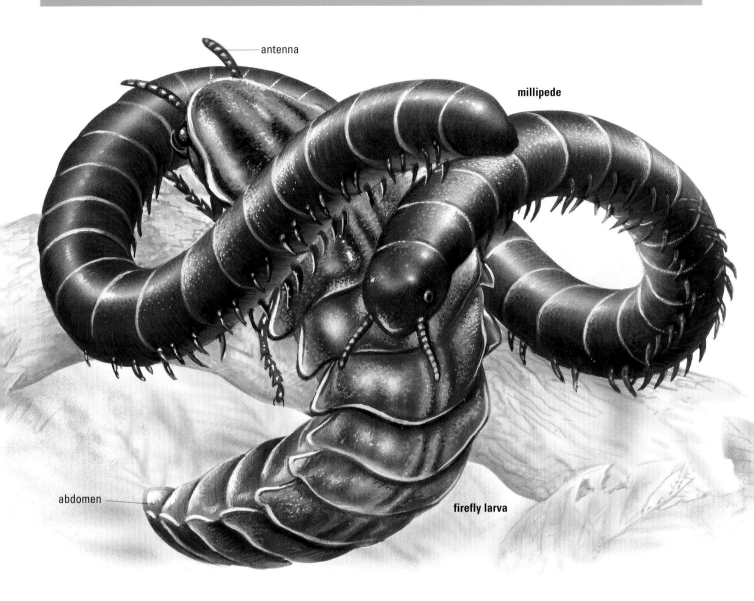

antenna

millipede

abdomen

firefly larva

these species may warn predators of their bad taste. Although it is not bioluminescent, at least one genus of cockroach in South America mimics the color and shape of fireflies to appear distasteful to predators. However, some birds, lizards, and frogs select fireflies as food, as do many invertebrates such as spiders, harvestmen, wasps, ants, and assassin bugs.

Fireflies and humans

Humans around the world have enjoyed the light shows produced by fireflies for centuries. These beetles have frequently appeared in works of art throughout the ages and are especially prominent in Asian cultures.

Scientists have exploited the biochemistry behind bioluminescence. Recent research has made use of the reaction between ATP and a mixture of luciferin and luciferase to provide a method for measuring HIV infection (HIV is the virus that causes AIDS.) This reaction is also used to monitor the progress of patients after cancer therapy, and there are many other medical applications.

Since ATP is crucially important to all organisms on Earth, exploratory spacecraft sometimes have a luciferin and luciferase mixture on board as a means of detecting extraterrestrial life. Samples are run through the mixture, and if ATP (and therefore a living organism) is present, light will be emitted.

▲ *Firefly larvae prey upon a range of other invertebrates, including millipedes.*

SEE ALSO
- *Beetle*
- *Communication*
- *Gnat*
- *Mimicry*
- *Senses*

FLEA

Fleas are parasitic insects that live on a variety of warm-blooded animals. Because they are carriers of the bacterium that causes plague, flea infestation led to the catastrophic "Black Death" in Europe and Asia during the 14th century.

Anyone who has lived with a cat or dog will be familiar with fleas and will probably at one time or another have spent money trying to get rid of these small insects. Because cats and dogs live in houses, the fleas that they carry are brought to people's attention, as they can irritate pets and can also bite people. However, fleas affect many wild

▼ *This picture was taken through a scanning electron microscope. The long hind legs power the flea's long leaps.*

mammals, too. In fact, there are around 2,000 species of fleas, which live all over the world, feeding on the blood of mammals and, in some cases, birds.

The master jumpers
Fleas are very small, at only 0.06 to 0.12 inches (1.5 to 3 mm) long. They belong to the insect order Siphonaptera, which

FLEA LIFE CYCLE

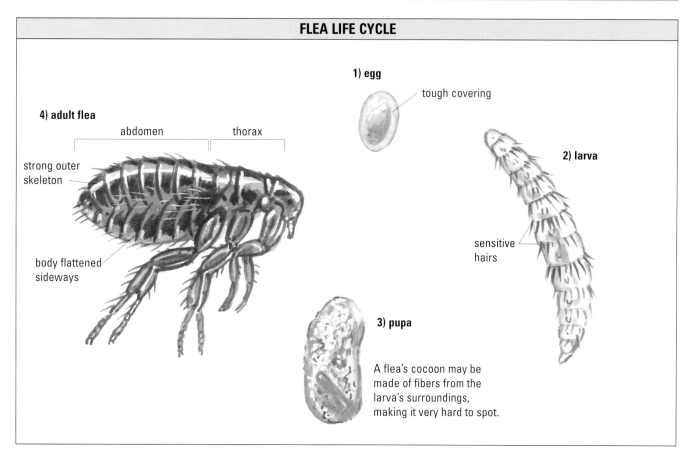

1) egg
tough covering

4) adult flea
abdomen   thorax

strong outer skeleton

2) larva

sensitive hairs

body flattened sideways

3) pupa

A flea's cocoon may be made of fibers from the larva's surroundings, making it very hard to spot.

---

means "sucking" and "wingless" in Greek. As the name suggests, they have no wings and therefore cannot fly, and adult fleas are parasites that feed by sucking blood through the skin of warm-blooded animals.

Instead of flying, fleas move around in great leaps using their powerful legs. Despite their small size, fleas can jump up to 7 inches (18 cm) into the air and 13 inches (33 cm) across the ground—a leap that is almost 150 times their body length. This is like a human jumping the length of a football field. When they leave the ground, fleas accelerate 50 times faster than the space shuttle.

Adaptations for parasitism

The body of a flea is perfectly designed for the type of life that it leads. To help it achieve its enormous jumps, a flea's hind legs are much longer than the other two pairs, and are even long compared to the rest of the body. The insect's exoskeleton (outer covering) is very strong and light, protecting the flea from

injury when it touches down on the ground after a jump. The covering is also waterproof, making fleas very tough little insects.

Fleas also have a flat body shape, as though their sides have been squashed together. The insect's antennae are extremely short, fitting neatly into grooves on the head. This helps them move around easily within the dense fur of the host (the animal on which they live). The color of adult fleas varies from yellow to almost black, depending on the species. Cat and dog fleas are a dark, reddish brown.

The mouthparts of adult fleas have evolved to have three separate functions. First, they are used to pierce the host's skin and draw blood. Next, the mouthparts are used to squirt saliva into the wound to digest the blood, and finally the flea uses its mouthparts to suck up the resulting mixture. This method of feeding is the reason that fleas have the potential to pass diseases between animals.

▲ *The life cycle of a flea. Fleas undergo complete metamorphosis, turning from a larva into an adult in the same way that a caterpillar becomes a butterfly.*

KEY FACTS

Name
Oriental rat flea (*Xenopsylla cheopis*)

Breeding
Female mates once and lays up to 50 eggs a day

Size
0.06 to 0.12 inches (1.5 to 3 mm) long

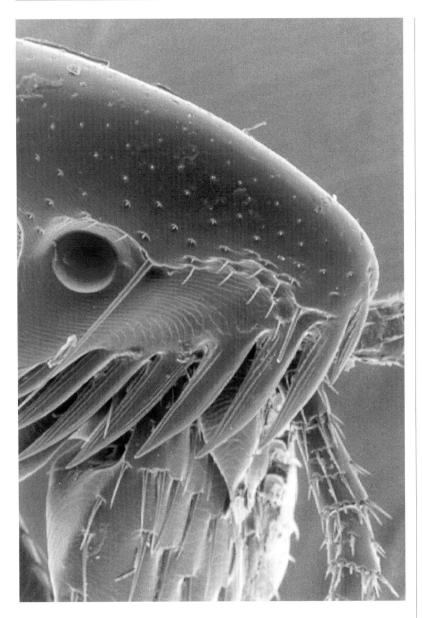

the animal and drop off when the animal moves around. The number of eggs builds up dramatically in places where the host spends much of its time. The dens of wild mammals may have extremely high numbers of eggs. It is thought that fleas can reach such high numbers that they may drive some animals, like badgers, out of their dens. In the same way, many eggs end up dropping to the floor of dog kennels or the sleeping boxes of cats.

Within a few days, the eggs hatch into larvae, which develop while hiding in cracks and crevices. Indoors, this may be between floorboards, in couches, or under rugs. Outdoors, they tend to be found in sandy soils or gravel. The larvae look like small, hairy worms and are completely blind. At this stage, they do not drink blood, but instead they have chewing mouthparts that they use to eat dead skin, hair, adult flea feces (which contain half-digested blood), or other, smaller parasites the larvae can find around them.

The fleas grow through three larval stages, getting larger at each stage. In some species, the larvae live for only about one week before they pupate, weaving themselves a silken cocoon. In other species, the flea may spend the winter as a larva in an inactive state before pupating in spring.

▲ *A colored electron micrograph of the head of a cat flea. The red object is the eye; the sharp structures are used to cut into the skin of the host.*

The flea life cycle

Adult female fleas breed once and start laying eggs after a meal of blood, and they may lay 15 to 50 eggs on the host every day of their life. The tiny white eggs are laid loosely within the coat of

Finding a host

Inside the cocoon, the flea changes from a larva into an adult over the course of a week or so. Adult fleas can live for months in this cocoon, but they can survive only for a few days

The flea kneels down on its hind legs.

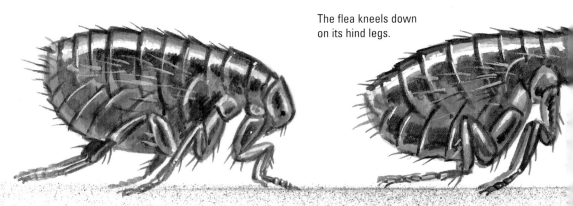

without feeding on blood when they emerge. Therefore, they tend to stay inside the cocoon until they sense that a food source is near.

A number of different things can trigger fleas into thinking that there is food nearby, making them emerge from the pupa. Heat, noise, pressure, such as from a pet lying down, and vibrations are all signs that there is an animal around that could be jumped on and fed upon. Fleas can also detect the presence of carbon dioxide, a gas that is present in the breath of a mammal when it exhales. When the fleas feel heat or vibration or detect carbon dioxide, the insects quickly jump toward the source and attempt to land on the host animal as it passes by.

The Black Death

From a human point of view, the most infamous of these insects is the Oriental rat flea. This species was the carrier of the bacteria that caused the plague epidemic known by historians as the "Black Death," which swept across Europe and Asia killing 25 million people in the 1350s. Roughly one-tenth of the entire population of the world died due to the disease. Many people became ill after being bitten

Flea takeoff

Scientists have only recently worked out how tiny fleas can make such remarkably long jumps. Fleas use a very springy protein in the skeleton around their thorax (midbody) to achieve their giant leaps. The very strong muscles used by most insects for flying are used by the flea to pull in the thorax, much like squeezing a coiled spring.

The flea raises its hind legs so it is balancing on its knees. It is now ready to jump. When the insect becomes aware of a nearby animal, it relaxes its flight muscles so the thorax springs back into its normal position. The force released by the springy skeleton travels down the hind legs and hits the ground, flinging the flea into the air with the acceleration that is greater than that of a space rocket.

by hungry Oriental rat fleas that had a population of plague bacteria in their digestive systems.

The fleas pick up the bacteria by feeding on the blood of an already infected rat or other animal. The bacteria then begin reproducing inside the flea's stomach, eventually blocking it and stopping the flea from digesting its food. This causes the fleas to behave as if they have not eaten; they begin biting their rat hosts more often and move on to humans. The plague bacteria are injected into the bite with the flea saliva, entering the bloodstream, and symptoms of the disease soon

hind legs

The hind legs straighten quickly.

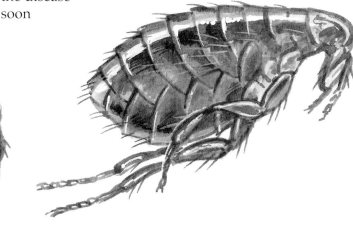

The flea is able to leap great distances. Often it will tumble through the air. The flea sticks out its clawed feet, helping it cling to the landing surface.

▲ *A diagram of a flea jumping into the air. The force of the jumps causes a clicking sound.*

follow. During the Black Death, fleas passed the disease from person to person and to other animals such as rats. Almost all of the people who caught the plague from flea bites died.

Today, because of medicine that can fight such diseases, the impact of fleas is not as serious. However, the insects can still cause problems. They get into houses by hopping in from the yard, or they can hitch a ride on an animal, including a human visitor. Because they can survive as larvae or pupae for a long time without food, fleas can lie dormant even if a house is empty for months and reappear when a new family moves in. They carry tiny parasitic worms as well as other disease-causing organisms, so it is important to keep pets free of fleas.

Some people are allergic to flea saliva and bites can result in an itchy skin. Controlling and getting rid of fleas is a difficult job. In very bad infestations, pesticides have to be used, but these must be applied by professionals.

▶ *The end of a flea's foreleg seen through an electron miscroscope. Claws at the end of the leg help the flea cling to the fur of the host.*

SEE ALSO

- *Biting louse*
- *Disease carrier*
- *Locomotion*
- *Metamorphosis*
- *Sucking louse*

▼ *A close-up of a flea sucking blood through human skin. This insect is so tiny it would look like a speck of dirt.*

FLY

The flies are one of the most successful of all animal groups. They live in almost all parts of the globe and have a wide range of body shapes and colors. Some species spread deadly diseases to humans and animals.

Nearly all living insects have wings or had an ancestor that had wings. However, not all flying insects are flies. Biologists recognize true flies by the number of wings they have. Most other flying insects have four wings, but flies only have two. The scientific name for the group, Diptera, means "two wings."

The flies are an incredibly successful group of insects. There are more than 20,000 species of flies living in North America alone, and worldwide there may be more than a million. They live in forests and deserts, on mountaintops and remote islands, in caves, and even over the sea.

▼ *A common housefly feeding on pineapple. The fly tastes the food through organs on its feet before dribbling saliva onto it that breaks down the food.*

Acrobatic experts
The wings of flies are designed for midair acrobatics. Hover flies suck nectar from flowers while hovering in the air. To do this, they beat their wings at up to 350 times per second. Many flies can fly sideways and backward or change direction very quickly. When in the air, they use two tiny clublike

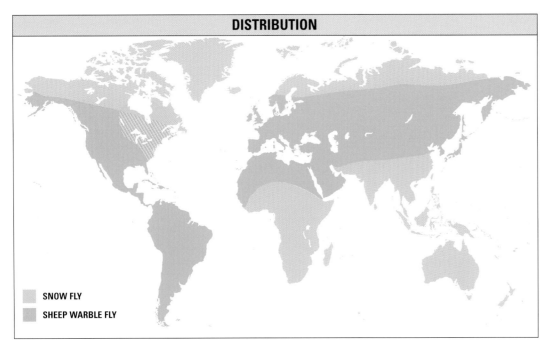

DISTRIBUTION

SNOW FLY

SHEEP WARBLE FLY

▶ *A dung fly takes to the air. The leap from the legs is immediately followed by a downstroke from the wings, which propels the insect forward and upward.*

structures called halteres that help the fly balance. Entomologists (people who study insects) believe that the first flies had four wings, and the halteres evolved from the second pair.

Flies are not only the most acrobatic of insects, but they are among the fastest fliers. Botflies have been timed traveling through the air at 25 mph (40 km/h). The aerial ability of flies is just one of the reasons for their incredible success.

Birds and bats flap their wings using muscles attached to the arm bones. Flies do things a little differently, using indirect muscular action. Rather than attaching directly to the wing, the flight muscles instead connect to the inside wall of the thorax (midbody). When they contract, the wall is bent inward, raising the wing; when the muscles relax, the opposite occurs. Flies save energy with this arrangement, since the elastic properties of the thorax wall and the muscles lower the amount of energy needed to flap the wings.

Flies large and small

Flies span a wide range of sizes. Crane flies have the longest wings. Some tropical species have a wingspan of almost 4 inches (10 cm). However, not all crane flies have large wings. Snow flies lack wings and resemble six-legged spiders. Among the largest flies are the robber and mydas flies, both of which can be nearly 3 inches (8 cm) long. By contrast, some species of biting midges are nearly fifty times smaller, at only about 0.04 inches (1 mm) long. These blood-sucking insects may be tiny but their bite can be very painful.

Feeding

Flies eat many things, from rotting flesh and nectar to living insects and garbage. Each group of flies has mouthparts adapted for the type of food it eats. This wide range of feeding habits is

KEY FACTS

Name
Snow fly
(*Chionea valga*)

Distinctive features
Long, slender legs; wingless but has halteres

Behavior
Walks on snow on cool winter days

Range
North America and Europe

Size
0.25 inches (7 mm)

◀ *The head of a fly. Flies have compound eyes. These are made up of many tiny lenses and are particularly good for picking up movement.*

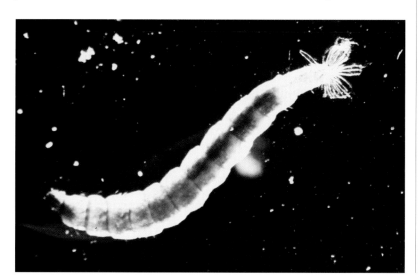

▼ *An aquatic fly larva. Some aquatic larvae use gills to absorb oxygen from the water. Others breathe air through tubes extending from the abdomen.*

another factor that has helped the group become so successful. Mosquitoes suck blood from birds and mammals using long, needlelike mouthparts.

Houseflies use their spongelike mouthparts to mop up partially digested food. Bee flies feed on the nectar produced by flowers, sucking it up through a long, tubelike proboscis.

Robber flies are fierce predators and stab their short mouthparts into other insects to suck out the juices from within. Nonbiting midges have poorly developed mouthparts and do not feed as adults, living for only a week or so. However, the larvae live much longer and must eat enough for themselves and the flying adult stage. Some flies, such as the horse botfly, live inside the gut of other animals as larvae before emerging as free-living adults.

The fly life cycle

Like many insects, flies have a four-stage life cycle. It begins when an adult female lays eggs. Larvae hatch from the eggs and feed for a time before becoming pupae. The adult flies eventually emerge from the pupae.

The adults and larvae are very different from each other and live in separate habitats. Larvae of many crane flies live in moss, rotting wood, soil, sand, mud, and water. They have pseudopods (false legs) and well-developed heads, and they feed on plants. Some crane fly larvae are called leatherjackets because of their thick brown skins. Other flies have larvae with no legs and simpler heads. These larvae are called maggots.

ANATOMY OF A FLY

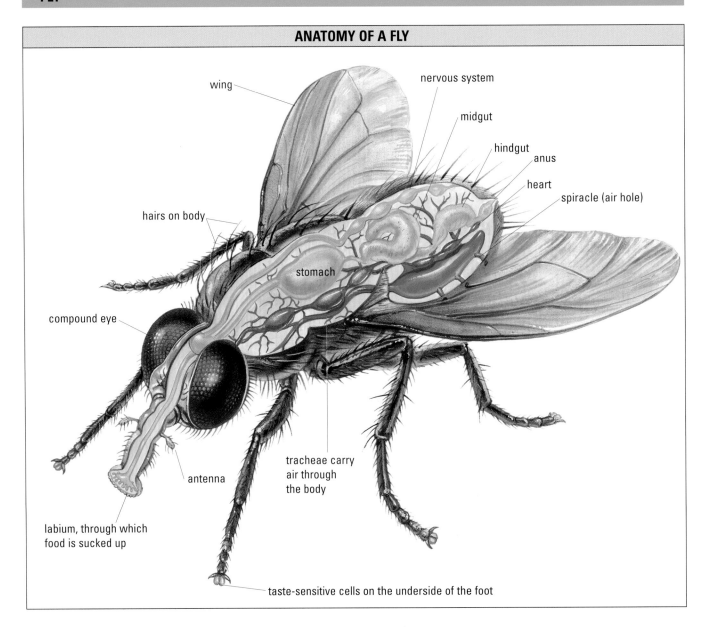

wing

nervous system

midgut

hindgut

anus

heart

spiracle (air hole)

hairs on body

stomach

compound eye

tracheae carry
air through
the body

antenna

labium, through which
food is sucked up

taste-sensitive cells on the underside of the foot

▲ *The anatomy of a house fly. The main difference between flies and other insects is the number of wings; most insects have four, but flies have only two.*

The tiny maggots of fruit flies are also herbivores (plant eaters). They feed on rotting fruit, leaves, and fungi. However, not all fly larvae feed on plants. Blowflies have large maggots that sometimes feed on living animals, including sheep, cattle, and people. Maggots of the closely related warble flies feed on domestic animals. They burrow deep inside the bodies of large mammals like horses and cows. When they are ready to pupate, they wriggle to the surface and burst out from the skin of the animal, causing sores.

Many larvae are adapted to live in extreme environments. The rat-tailed maggot is a type of larval hover fly and is common in stagnant water with little oxygen. It crawls along the bottom on its pseudopods and breathes through a long siphon that sticks out of the water like a giant snorkel. Brine fly larvae can live in the harshest of environments. They inhabit salt water and hot springs. One species, the petroleum fly, lives in water floating on top of natural pools of oil. Petroleum flies live only around the oil fields of California.

Laying eggs

Fly larvae are good at eating but cannot move very far. As a result, the adults generally lay their eggs near a food source for the larvae. Mosquito larvae

live in pools of water, but the adults cannot swim. Some species overcome this problem by releasing their eggs in the air so they drop into the water. Others lay them on land and let rain wash them into the pools.

Larvae of tachinid flies live on the bodies of insects and other arthropods, while bat flies live only on the bodies of bats. For parasites, finding another animal to lay eggs on wastes energy. To counter this, the human botfly, or torsalo, of South America catches mammal-biting flies (such as mosquitoes) in midair and attaches its eggs to their bodies. When the flies land on a

▲ *A greenbottle fly feeding. Powerful muscles in the head contract to suck in the liquid food.*

▼ *Some flies are beneficial. This Thrypticus fly was discovered recently in South America, and it is now used in the biological control of the weed water hyacinth.*

suitable mammal, the newly hatched botfly larvae burrow into the mammal's skin. Some parasitic fly larvae ambush their hosts. The eggs are laid on the ground, and the larvae wait on damp vegetation for a passing spider. They leap up and attach themselves to the body of the spider. The larvae then slowly eat their way in through the spider's outer skin before feeding on its internal organs.

Flies and people

People do not like flies because they bite and sometimes spread diseases. Black-flies are said to have the most painful bite of any fly. During certain seasons, people in some parts of Africa have to stay inside during the day to avoid being bitten by huge swarms of these bloodsuckers. The bite of the blackfly is not only very painful but can contain tiny worms that may cause people to become blind. Mosquitoes carry a range of disease-causing organisms, including malaria. Even the housefly can spread cholera, dysentry, and typhoid.

A number of flies are harmless to humans as adults but have flesh-eating maggots. For example, the Congo floor maggot lives on the ground in some African forests, and will suck the blood of sleeping humans and other animals.

The rarest fly in North America

Most flies are relatively common. However, some are extremely rare. Only one North American fly is listed as endangered. This is the Delhi-sands flower-loving fly.

This species is limited to 12 sites in southern California, containing a total of around 500 individuals. The flies are around 1 inch (2.5 cm) long and are striped orange and dark brown. It is a bee-mimicking species.

The adults feed on flower nectar, but what the larvae feed on is unknown. The males are strong fliers, but the females only fly occasionally. The Delhi-sands flower-loving fly has become rare as it has lost habitat to building works and because of fires and illegal garbage dumping. The fly is now the subject of a conservation program.

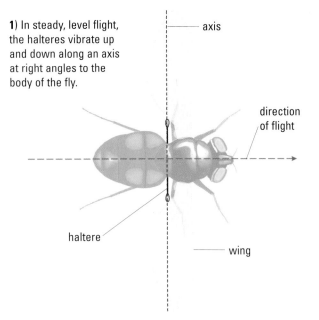

1) In steady, level flight, the halteres vibrate up and down along an axis at right angles to the body of the fly.

axis

direction of flight

haltere

wing

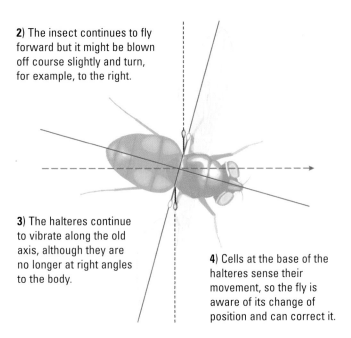

2) The insect continues to fly forward but it might be blown off course slightly and turn, for example, to the right.

3) The halteres continue to vibrate along the old axis, although they are no longer at right angles to the body.

4) Cells at the base of the halteres sense their movement, so the fly is aware of its change of position and can correct it.

▲ *How the halteres help control stability during flight in flies.*

▶ *Some insects, such as this horse-fly, require a blood meal before laying their eggs.*

Flies can be helpful

Flies are considered to be pests because they bite and infect farm animals and their larvae eat crops. However, many flies are useful to farmers. In some orchards, hover flies pollinate more flowers than the bees they imitate. Their larvae are also important because they eat aphids, caterpillars, and other pests.

Some people like to eat flies. In east Africa, midges gather above lakes in huge numbers. The local people used to trap millions of these minute insects and press them together to form a food called kungu cake. Brine flies are abundant around the shores of Lake Mono in California, and Native Americans used to gather up and eat large numbers of

their pupae. Other flies have had important symbolic roles. In ancient Eygpt, predatory robber flies were a symbol of bravery in battle.

Essential to the ecosystem

Flies are important in every terrestrial (land-based) ecosystem. They provide food for a wide range of animals. Some animals are adapted to eat only flies. The adults even provide some plants, like the Venus flytrap, with the nutrients they need. Larvae that feed on rotting meat help spread the nutrients throughout the environment.

Abundance and extreme rarity

Eurychoromyia mallea is an unusual fly because it has a head shaped like a hammer. It is also the rarest known fly. It is known from only four adults that were collected by one person in the same place in 1903. No other individuals of this species have ever been found. It is so different from other types of flies that entomologists put it in a family of its own called the broad-headed flies. The whole family may now be extinct. Other flies are extremely common. The housefly has lived alongside people for thousands of years. Today it prospers, feeding on garbage and other waste.

FRUIT FLY

Many fruit fly species are very important to human activities.

Some are pests and can have devastating effects on fruit crops.

Other fruit flies, however, have become vital research tools.

The term fruit fly is commonly applied to flies from two different families. Vinegar or pomace flies feed on the yeast that develops on rotting fruit and vegetables. They are well known for their role in scientific research. Peacock flies are common pests of fruit and vegetable crops, causing a great deal of damage to these plants.

Genetic research

Vinegar flies live around the world, including most of the United States. There are more than 3,000 species, but one species, *Drosophila melanogaster*, has the closest link to humans. For more than a century, this fly (usually just called *Drosophila*) has been used in genetics research. It is ideally suited to the task, because it is small—about 0.1 inches (2.5 mm) long—and is easily raised in bottles, where it is fed on a mixture of molasses and yeast. A single pair of *Drosophila* can produce hundreds of offspring, which become adults themselves in less than three weeks.

Drosophila have many visible characteristics, such as the color of the eyes or body, the size of their wings, and the shape and distribution of bristles on the body, that are controlled by a single gene. A gene is a part of a DNA (deoxyribonucleic acid) molecule that controls the development of a particular characteristic. Genes can be passed on to offspring, and *Drosophila* are used in experiments that test how characteristics change when genes are altered.

▼ *A vinegar fly feeds on fruit juice bubbling through the skin of an orange. These flies often feed on rotting fruit, vegetables, and bread.*

KEY FACTS

Name
Medfly
(*Ceratitis capitata*)

Distinctive features
Brightly colored wings, complex courtship display

Feeding
Adult eats nectar and sap; larva feeds on fruit pulp

Size
Less than 0.4 inches (1 cm) long

DISTRIBUTION

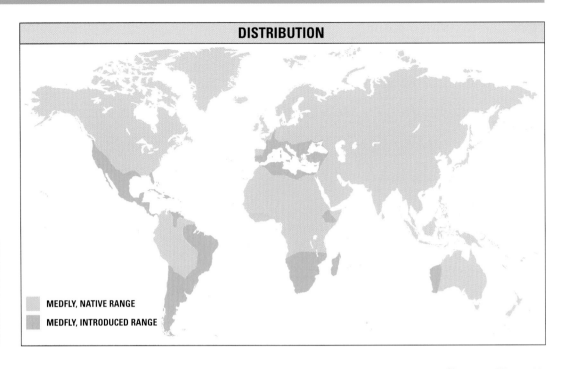

MEDFLY, NATIVE RANGE
MEDFLY, INTRODUCED RANGE

▼ *Two of these* Drosophila *flies have mutant genes. Scientists study these genes to learn more about how they control a fly's development.*

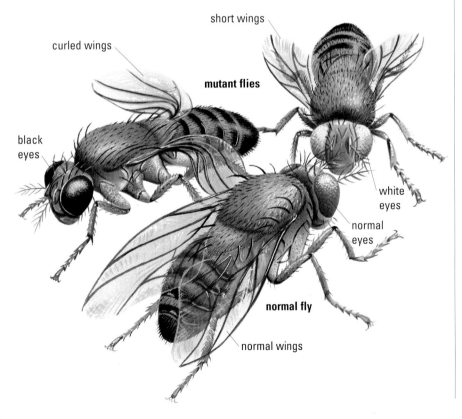

short wings

curled wings

mutant flies

black eyes

white eyes

normal eyes

normal fly

normal wings

Scientists now know about every *Drosophila* gene and have bred many strains with unusual characteristics.

Vinegar flies in the wild

Today *Drosophila* and other vinegar flies are found in the wild all over the world. These flies are common across the United States, especially in Hawaii, where there are more than 800 different species. This abundance, together with the isolation of Hawaii from the mainland, allows scientists to study how new species may be developing.

Vinegar flies are often found around garbage cans and dumps, where the adults and larvae feed on rotting vegetable matter. These flies are also particularly attracted to yeast-filled foods such as bread and alcohol.

During courtship, a male vinegar fly sings by vibrating his wings very rapidly. This singing attracts a female, who selects the male with the most impressive performance. After mating, the female lays about 500 eggs in the remaining two or three weeks of her life.

Peacock flies

The peacock flies are also referred to by experts as true fruit flies. They derive their name from their colorful wings and extravagant mating displays. There are more than 4,000 species of peacock flies, which live around the world. Perhaps the best-known species of peacock fly is the Mediterranean fruit fly, or medfly, which evolved in the warm west African tropical region but has been transported around the world

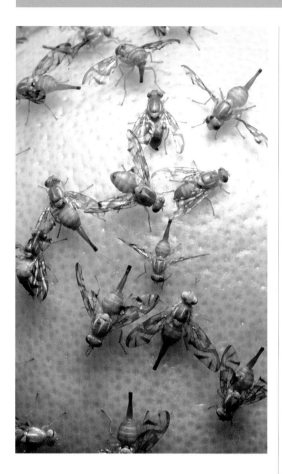

with the export of fruit and vegetables. The medfly feeds on more than 250 varieties of fruits and vegetables, including crops such as citrus fruits and tomatoes. In the area around the Mediterranean Sea, some harvests have been completely wiped out by medflies.

The medfly life cycle

The male medfly produces a female-attracting pheromone (chemical) from a gland in his abdomen. He vibrates his wings to help spread the pheromone through the air. When the female approaches, the two flies spread their wings and circle one another. It was this behavior that first led scientists to compare these flies to peacocks. When the female is satisfied with the display, she allows the male to mate with her.

The female then pierces the skin of a fruit with her sharp ovipositor (egg tube) and lays up to ten eggs in each fruit. After two or three days, the eggs hatch and the maggots (wormlike larvae) begin to feed on the fruit pulp.

◀ *Female Mexican fruit flies lay their eggs inside a grapefruit. The fly larvae may be carried all over the world inside the fruit.*

▼ *A medfly lays its eggs inside the soft outer layer of a ripe coffee berry.*

When they are fully grown, the maggots leave the fruit and drop to the ground. They pupate (change from a larva to an adult) beneath the surface of the soil and emerge after about ten days. The full life cycle takes around 30 days, so a fruit crop can be repeatedly affected throughout a single growing season.

Controlling medflies

Medflies are not strong fliers, but they have spread far and wide through the transportation of fruit containing medfly larvae. This fly has entered the United States several times—most often in Florida, California, and Hawaii. In such vulnerable areas, pheromone-baited traps are set to reveal the presence of the flies. Strict quarantine measures restrict the movement of fruit and other crops, helping prevent the spread of the pest. The ground beneath fruit trees can also be treated with insecticide to kill the larvae as they burrow underground. In some affected places, males are sterilized by radiation and released in large numbers. These males breed with the females, but no fertilized eggs are laid as a result, leading to a swift decline in the local population.

FUNNEL-WEB SPIDER

Funnel-web spiders are among the most venomous and dangerous spiders. These spiders stab their prey with sharp fangs by raising and lowering their bodies.

Funnel-web spiders belong to a group called the mygalomorphs. Although they look similar to other spiders, mygalomorphs differ in many ways. The fangs of most spiders close together from the side, allowing the spider to bite its prey. Mygalomorph fangs are different and point downward from the tip of the jawlike chelicerae. Therefore, these spiders can stab their prey but cannot bite them.

To generate momentum for the stab, the spider raises its body, extends the fangs, and then strikes forward. They also differ from other spiders by having two pairs of book lungs (gas-exchange surfaces)—other spiders have only one. In addition, female mygalomorphs continue to molt after they reach adulthood, something that is extremely rare in other spiders.

Funnel-web spiders live throughout tropical regions and in some cooler areas. They are particularly diverse in

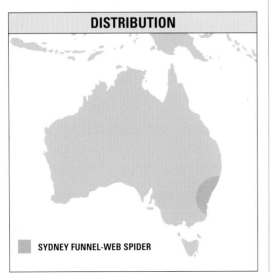

DISTRIBUTION

■ SYDNEY FUNNEL-WEB SPIDER

Australia. One Australian species, the Sydney funnel-web spider, is large and glossy black, with large fangs. They build funnel-shaped silken retreats in sheltered places, under logs and rocks, and often in back yards. Lines of silk stream from the entrance to form a sheet web, and the spiders ambush prey that blunders in. This includes beetles, cockroaches, snails, and even vertebrates such as frogs and mice.

Sydney funnel-web spiders are particularly long-lived, and it may take up to eight years before they become adults. After this, the female may live for many more years, but the males have a shorter time in which to find a mate before they die. The females spend their entire lives in their funnels, while the males wander in search of a mate. They are guided by pheromones released by the female.

▲ *A Sydney funnel-web spider in a threat posture, with its large fangs clearly on display.*

KEY FACTS

Name
Spruce-fir moss spider (*Microhexura montivaga*)

Distinctive features
Very small spider; male has spurs on forelegs

Habitat
Forest moss mats

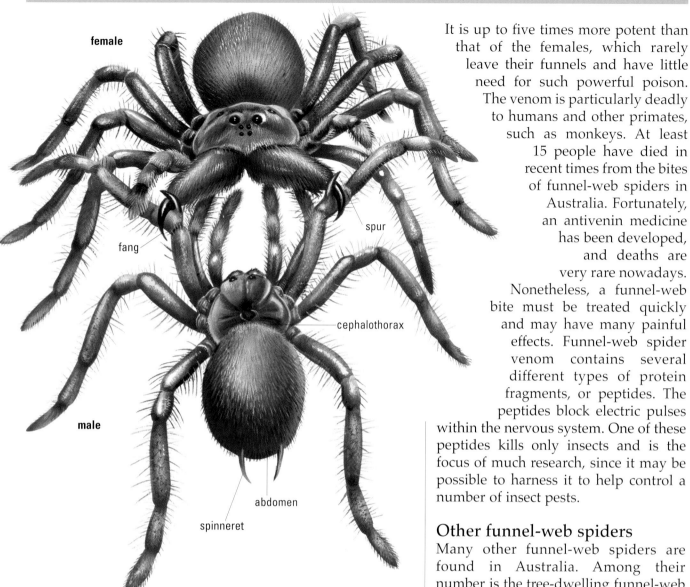

female

fang

spur

male

cephalothorax

abdomen

spinneret

It is up to five times more potent than that of the females, which rarely leave their funnels and have little need for such powerful poison. The venom is particularly deadly to humans and other primates, such as monkeys. At least 15 people have died in recent times from the bites of funnel-web spiders in Australia. Fortunately, an antivenin medicine has been developed, and deaths are very rare nowadays. Nonetheless, a funnel-web bite must be treated quickly and may have many painful effects. Funnel-web spider venom contains several different types of protein fragments, or peptides. The peptides block electric pulses within the nervous system. One of these peptides kills only insects and is the focus of much research, since it may be possible to harness it to help control a number of insect pests.

Other funnel-web spiders

Many other funnel-web spiders are found in Australia. Among their number is the tree-dwelling funnel-web spider. This spider lives deep in the forest, and it rarely comes into contact with humans. This is fortunate because its venom is even more toxic than that of the Sydney funnel-web.

Funnel-web spiders are uncommon in the United States. However, several nonvenomous species live in the Southwest. Another U.S. species is the endangered spruce-fir moss spider. At only 0.2 inches (5 mm) long, this species is the smallest of all the funnel-web spiders. The tiny spider is found in just a few places in the Appalachian Mountains, where it is lives on damp mats of moss. It is difficult for this spider to spread to new areas, and with the decline of its high-altitude forest habitat, this species is now very rare.

When threatened, the males adopt a raised attacking posture. Due to their aggressive nature and potent venom, male Sydney funnel-webs are one of the most dangerous spiders to humans. They do occasionally come into homes when looking for a mate.

When the male finds a female, he weaves a silken mat, onto which he deposits sperm. During mating, the male uses a spur on his second leg to hold the female's fangs, which stops her from stabbing him with them.

Funnel-web venom

The males are at great risk of predation as they wander. They counter this by having a venom of staggering toxicity.

▲ *Male mygalomorphs often have a pair of spurs on the forelegs. Many use these to hold the female's fangs during mating, while others hold the legs of the female in place.*

SEE ALSO
- *Spider*
- *Tarantula*
- *Trap-door spider*

GIANT EARWIG

The largest species of earwig lives on the remote island of St. Helena. This magnificent insect has not been seen alive for more than 30 years, however, and entomologists fear it may already have become extinct.

The St. Helena giant earwig is the world's largest earwig. It was first discovered in 1798, but it was lost to science until its rediscovery in 1965. Giant earwigs seek shelter under stones during the day. They become active at night or during summer rains when temperatures are cooler.

Giant earwigs probably feed on both plants and animals. They mate between December and February, and females begin laying and guarding their eggs in March. Adult giant earwigs can be up to 3 inches (76 mm) long, including their forceps. They are black, with reddish legs, short wing covers, and are wingless. The forceps are exceptionally long, up to one-third of the total body length. The females are a little smaller, with shorter forceps. Giant earwigs are restricted to a small area of St. Helena, a tiny, remote island in the south Atlantic.

The last living specimens were found on Horse Point Plain, in the northeastern part of the island. The landscape there is very dry and rocky, dotted with

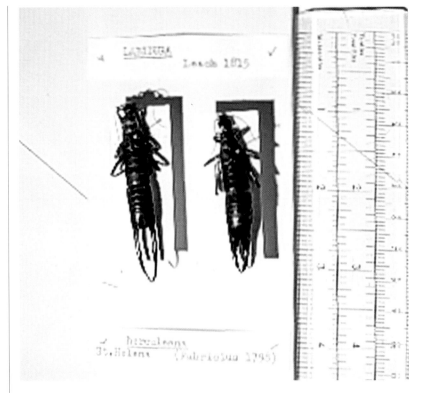

scattered tufts of grass and the occasional shrub. The last forty giant earwigs ever seen alive were collected by a team of Belgian scientists between 1965 and 1967. Although considered relatively common at the time, the scientists recognized the possibility of the giant earwig becoming extinct. Many native animals on St. Helena, including all but one of the land birds, have disappeared since the island was discovered in the early sixteenth century by Portuguese sailors.

Recent surveys by entomologists of the area have failed to find any giant earwigs at all, and it is possible that this magnificent insect is now lost forever.

▲ *These pinned giant earwigs are among the few specimens that are known to exist. The ruler shows just how large these insects are. The specimen on the right is female.*

SEE ALSO

- *Earwig*
- *Endangered species*

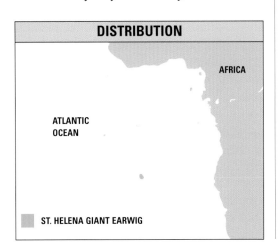

DISTRIBUTION

AFRICA

ATLANTIC OCEAN

■ ST. HELENA GIANT EARWIG

GLASSWING BUTTERFLY

These rain forest butterflies are very difficult to spot, since they have transparent wings and can blend into any background.

Glasswing butterflies are named for their delicate transparent wings. They live in the shrubs that grow on the floor of tropical forests in South America and around the Caribbean Sea. Glasswings belong to a butterfly family called clearwings, but some other butterflies with see-through wings are also referred to as glasswings.

A clear membrane

Glasswings are typically small, with thin antennae, a slender abdomen, and long, rounded wings divided into transparent areas by veins. The forewings are larger than the hind wings.

Butterfly wings are covered in scales, which give them their colors. The scales of a glasswing are very small, hairlike and colorless, revealing the clear membrane beneath. The transparent wings of the windowpane butterfly are marked with black veins and bluish patches. Like most glasswings, it inhabits gloomy forests and seldom ventures into direct sunlight. Glasswings have

evolved transparent wings as a result of living in their shady habitat. Colors are of little use in the dark, and the glasswings' transparent wings provide excellent camouflage against predators such as birds.

Toxic caterpillars

Most glasswing caterpillars are slender, smooth, and pale colored but some have darker stripes. All clearwing caterpillars live on tropical plants belonging to the nightshade family, many of which contain poisonous chemicals.

Glasswing caterpillars protect themselves from predators by storing the plant poisons in their bodies, making them taste bad in a predator's mouth. The bodies of many adult butterflies also contain these chemicals.

▲ *A glasswing butterfly stands on a fern frond. The green fern can be seen through the insect's wings. The transparent wings make it very hard for a predator to spot a glasswing.*

SEE ALSO

- *Blue butterfly*
- *Coloration*
- *Moth and butterfly*
- *Swallowtail*
- *White butterfly*

DISTRIBUTION

GLASSWING BUTTERFLIES

GNAT

Gnats are small, two-winged flies that often bite or annoy people. Some are able to produce light as larvae. The name *gnat* applies to many species from several different families.

All gnats are flies, and belong to the insect group called the Diptera. Gnats have mouthparts adapted for sucking juices, from plants or animals. Many drink blood, and some are serious pests. The word *gnat* has no precise scientific meaning, and these insects are not closely related, being scattered across several families of flies. In Britain, mosquitoes are often called gnats, while in the United States, people sometimes call fruit flies or biting midges gnats. Buffalo gnats infest livestock, sometimes in vast numbers, but are actually blackflies, as are the turkey gnats that attack poultry. The long-legged snow

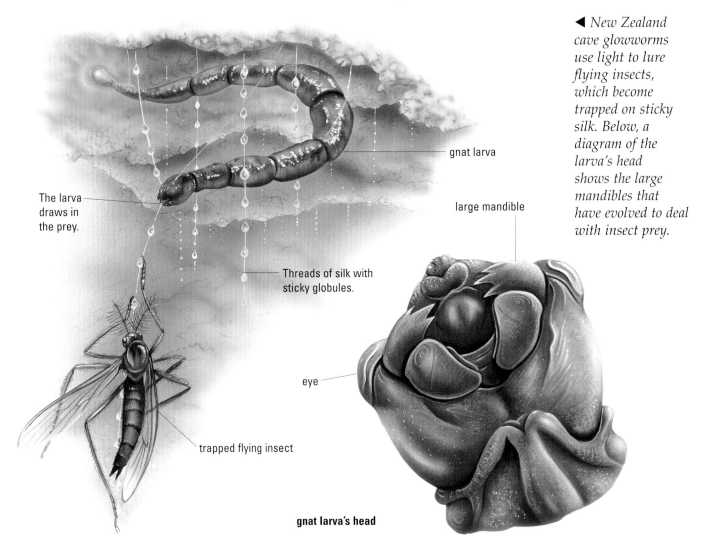

◄ New Zealand cave glowworms use light to lure flying insects, which become trapped on sticky silk. Below, a diagram of the larva's head shows the large mandibles that have evolved to deal with insect prey.

gnat larva

The larva draws in the prey.

Threads of silk with sticky globules.

trapped flying insect

large mandible

eye

gnat larva's head

gnats seen on mild winter days are actually crane flies. Gall gnats, whose larvae live inside swellings on the leaves of plants, are a type of midge.

Eye gnats

One of the more unpleasant types of gnat is the eye gnat. The larvae of these flies feed on decaying vegetation and dung, but the adults feed on animal secretions such as pus, blood, and mucus. They are particularly fond of the fluid around people's eyes. These gnats can transmit eye diseases such as yaws and conjunctivitis, and can even cause blindness in humans or animals.

Eye gnats belong to a small family of insects known as the frit flies or grass flies. These are most common in meadows and other grassy habitats. The larvae develop inside immature grain heads or in grass stems.

As well as feeding on wild grasses, the larvae also attack cultivated cereals such as oats, wheat, barley, and rye, and sometimes they cause great damage. The larvae of some species feed on the eggs of other insects and spiders. The adults are small, and some species are bright yellow and black.

Another disease-spreading gnat is the sand fly, which is found in warm, dry parts of the world. Female sand flies are bloodsuckers that prey on large warm-blooded animals, including humans.

▲ *Adult gall gnats mating. As larvae, these gnats attack the leaves of plants, which produce swellings, or galls, in response. The larvae live inside these galls.*

▼ *An adult eye gnat at rest. In many places these disease-spreading flies are a public health problem.*

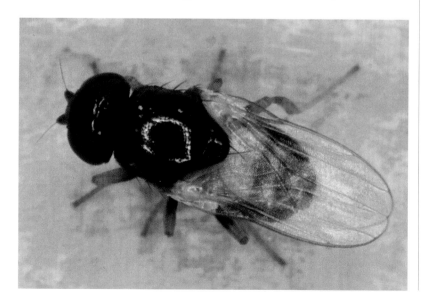

Wood and fungus gnats

Wood gnats are a small group of flies that includes nine North American species. They generally live on damp vegetation and are sometimes seen in huge swarms consisting entirely of males. The adults are attracted to the sap that flows from injured trees, and the larvae feed on fermenting sap and decaying vegetation.

Fungus gnats are so named because their larvae live in and feed on mushrooms and other fungi. They are found worldwide in damp places such as woods and caves, especially where rotting vegetation is common. The adults, which look like mosquitoes, are usually brown, black, or yellowish and have long legs and a characteristic "hunchback" formed by a bulge in the thorax (midbody). There are more than 600 species of fungus gnats in North America, many of which are very common. Fungus gnats lay their eggs in fungi, rotting wood, bird's nests, or on damp cave walls. Some species are a serious pest in mushroom farms. In other species, the larvae are predators. These larvae produce slimy webs of silk to ensnare insects, much as spiders do.

The sticky threads are sometimes covered with droplets of a poisonous secretion that helps to stun victims.

When a fly or other insect blunders into the trap, the larva emerges from a crevice or other hiding place, bites the prey to inject a venom, and then retreats with the meal into its shelter. Like spiders, fungus gnat larvae can overpower insects much larger than themselves, and they sometimes wrap up their victims in silk. This helps contain the victims' struggles.

Glowing in the dark

Some cave-dwelling fungus gnats have developed a remarkable means of luring prey into their traps. Species such as the New Zealand cave glowworm give out a dim light from their abdomens. This attracts flying insects, which are trapped on sticky webs that dangle from the roof of the cave.

The production of light by an organism is called bioluminescence. Only a dozen or so of the thousands of fungus gnat species are bioluminescent. Among these, all species glow as larvae and several retain their light-producing abilities as both pupae and adults.

The dark-winged fungus gnats, or root gnats, are darker in color than other fungus gnats but are otherwise similar. They also live in shady places and lay their eggs in fungi. These insects can become pests in mushroom farms. The larvae of other gnat species feed on the roots of plants and can damage root crops such as potatoes or plants grown in greenhouses or indoors. One species, the potato scab gnat, transmits a damaging plant disease called potato scab. Female potato scab gnats are easy to identify because they have extremely short wings and no halteres.

DISTRIBUTION

NEW ZEALAND CAVE GLOWWORM

▶ *Gnats gather on a grass stem. Gnats often aggregate in large numbers, swarming either to find a mate or to make use of a good food source.*

GRASSHOPPER AND CRICKET

Grasshoppers, crickets, and katydids are a diverse and widespread group. With powerful jumping legs, some species can leap distances of up to 10 feet (3 m). Some species are pests, and in large numbers they can devastate crops.

There are few places in the world where the calls of grasshoppers, katydids, and crickets cannot be heard during warm parts of the year. These insects belong to the order Orthoptera. All orthopterans have chewing mouthparts. Most members of the group are plant eaters, but a few feed on other insects for part of their diets.

Many orthopterans use sound to communicate. The songs are produced by rubbing the bases of the wings together or scraping the legs against the edges of the wings. This is called stridulation. Orthopterans have eardrums on their legs or abdomen. The forewings are slightly thickened and interlaced with veins, while the hind wings are broad, pleated, and kept folded.

Two main groups

With about 17,000 species around the world, the Orthoptera are divided into two suborders. One group includes the locusts and grasshoppers, which have short antennae and are active during the day. Crickets, mole crickets, and katydids make up the other suborder. These have threadlike antennae that are longer than the body, and they are nocturnal (active at night).

▲ This spike-headed katydid from the rain forests of the Amazon is well-protected by its spines, making it an unpleasant meal for a hungry bird or lizard.

The name *katydid* is derived from the call of the North American true katydid, which sounds like "katy-she-did."

Making sounds

Orthopterans produce sound mainly to attract mates. The pitch and pattern of the calls, usually produced by males, are unique to each species. Crickets and katydids rub sets of tiny pegs located at the base of one wing against a ridge on the other to produce clicks, buzzes, and chirps. The wing stroke varies between four and 200 times per second. The sound is amplified by a smooth membrane called a mirror, which is located on the base of the wing. The eardrums of these insects are located on the front legs. Male field crickets chirp to attract females and secure their territory. They position themselves facing toward

◀ A grasshopper resting on a twig. Its bright yellow coloration acts as a warning to predators that this insect is poisonous and does not make a tasty meal.

Plagues of locusts

Irruptions (invasions in large numbers) of locusts have ravaged crops in parts of Africa and the Middle East for thousands of years. Some of the earliest Sumerian writings (the Sumerian civilization flourished in northern Iraq around 6000 B.C.E.) mention them, and various religious texts tell of the plague suffered in Egypt around the time of Moses. Today, swarms of locusts still attack crops in large numbers, and sometimes they cause terrible famine.

For most of the time, locusts are camouflaged to match their surroundings and live alone. After a series of favorable seasons, however, the numbers of these "solitary" locusts build up, and crowding occurs. Newly hatched nymphs begin to look and act differently; these locusts are black and yellow and are very active, and are referred to as "gregarious" locusts. The locusts gather and may migrate to new, less crowded areas in a swarm. They fly until either it begins to rain or night falls, after which they land and begin to feed on whatever vegetation is available.

The cricket flaps its wings downward to keep aloft.

The back legs snap powerfully, propeling the insect into the air.

The delicate hind wings are kept beneath the tough forewings.

forewing

hind wing

Crickets and katydids typically have very long, thin antennae.

Singing grasshoppers

Grasshoppers sing by rubbing the femora, the longest segments of their hind legs, against the edges of the forewings. The sound is amplified (made louder) by expanding the wings. The eardrums of these insects are toward the rear of the abdomen. Some types of grasshoppers, such as the horse lubber grasshopper from southwestern North America, create sound by rapidly opening and closing their hind wings, bringing a series of rough-surfaced veins together. Band-wing grasshoppers make a crackling noise by folding and unfolding their hind wings.

Living thermometers

Grasshoppers are sensitive to temperature changes, and when the temperature rises, males produce their songs at a much faster rate. As each song is particular to a certain species, this could cause problems for some grasshoppers. However, females change their responses to the songs to match the changes in the temperature, so they are still able to recognize the calls of potential mates regardless of how warm or cold it is.

the entrance to their burrows, exposing their abdomens. The burrows are Y-shaped, and the two openings increase the distance the call travels.

Tree crickets live on vegetation and sing holding their wings at 90 degrees to the body, using nearby leaves to amplify their call. Some female katydids answer the calls of the male with a call of their own. Wingless species such as female Jerusalem crickets drum their abdomens on the ground to attract mrales.

▲ *A great green bush cricket jumps. Taking off from the ground requires a great deal of force from the hind legs to overcome gravity, especially for heavier insects. Long hind legs help generate this extra force.*

DISTRIBUTION

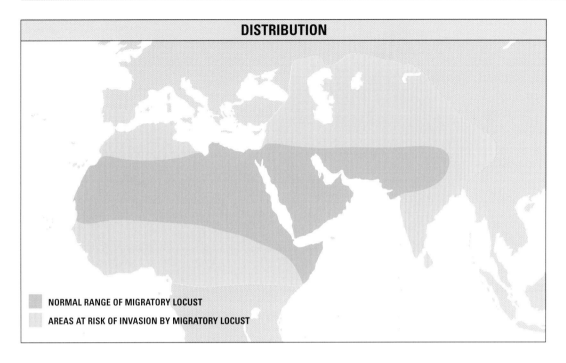

▨ NORMAL RANGE OF MIGRATORY LOCUST
▧ AREAS AT RISK OF INVASION BY MIGRATORY LOCUST

KEY FACTS

Name
True katydid
(*Pterophylla
camellofolia*)

**Distinctive
features**
Wings are leaflike;
female has a flat,
curved ovipositor

Behavior
Male calls to
female, which
answers with call
of its own

Breeding
Eggs laid in rotten
wood or soil in fall

Food
Shoots and leaves

Size
1.7 to 2.3 inches
(43 to 58 mm) long

Egg laying and development

Most female crickets and katydids have long ovipositors, egg-laying tubes designed to place eggs out of harm's way, deep into soil or rotting wood. However, the broad-wing katydid uses its wide, swordlike ovipositor to lay flat, seedlike eggs in overlapping rows on twigs. Mole crickets have no ovipositor and instead dig an underground chamber where they deposit and care for their eggs. Female grasshoppers also lack external ovipositors, but they have thickened valves on the tips of their abdomen. The female uses these to drill through the soil and uses the length of her entire abdomen to deposit the eggs. The eggs form pods held together with a sticky secretion. A few species attach their egg pods to vegetation, while others place them inside stems.

The eggs hatch in a few weeks. Hatching orthopterans (called nymphs) look like miniature versions of the adults but lack wings. They undergo between six and ten molts before becoming mature. Orthopterans molt at night, when the air is relatively moist. Prior to molting, the nymph anchors its claws onto a branch or leaf so that it is hanging upside down. It sucks in air, causing the new body inside to expand and rupture the old outer skin. The newly emerged insect might eat the old skin to save nutrients.

Enemies and defense

Orthopterans have developed numerous defensive strategies as well as flying and jumping. Potential predators and parasites often track their victims by following the calls of singing males. To avoid detection, some species, such as the female Jerusalem cricket, call through the soil to avoid giving away their position to hungry predators. Some grasshoppers have a high-pitched call. This makes it difficult for predators

▼ *A male and female grasshopper mating. Males of many orthopterans clasp the female using a pincer on the abdomen.*

to locate the source. Bats often feed on orthopterans that are active at night. Rather than using vision, bats rely on pulses of very high-pitched sound to find their way about and to locate their prey. Some types of katydids are able to hear these sounds. When they hear bats calling, the katydids stop singing and keep very still until the danger has passed.

African and South American katydids deter predators with their large size and spiny bodies. Others use camouflage, avoiding predators by blending in with leaves, sticks, stones, gravel, or sand. Many grasshoppers and crickets have strong mouthparts to help them deal with tough plant material, and some, such as coneheads, can give a nasty bite.

Some orthopterans mimic plants to avoid detection. Tropical katydids have wings that are remarkably similar to the shape, color, and texture of living or dead leaves, right down to their veins, blotches, and holes made by feeding insects. To complete the disguise, they sway gently back and forth, as if moved

---

KEY FACTS

Name
Horse lubber grasshopper (*Taeniopoda eques*)

Distinctive features
Black with yellow markings

Food
Plants and insects

Range
Southern United States

▼ *This great green bush cricket is eating a grasshopper. Although most orthopterans are plant eaters, some will feed on other insects.*

---

by a breeze. When caught, some grasshoppers squirt blood from the joints of the legs, startling the predator.

Colors and chemicals

Other species sport bold, bright markings to warn predators to stay away. The black, yellow, and orange markings of the horse lubber grasshopper advertise the fact that its body is filled with bitter tasting chemicals. Some African grasshoppers release a pungent foam from glands located in the thorax (midbody) that drives away predators.

Some Brazilian katydids mimic tarantula hawk wasps, which have deep metallic blue bodies and rust-red wings. They move like the wasps and will even pretend to sting when captured.

Agricultural pests

Plagues of crickets and grasshoppers have invaded homes and ravaged crops for centuries, and they are mentioned in many ancient texts. Migratory locusts can form enormous swarms in Africa and Asia and are capable of destroying

ANATOMY OF A LOCUST

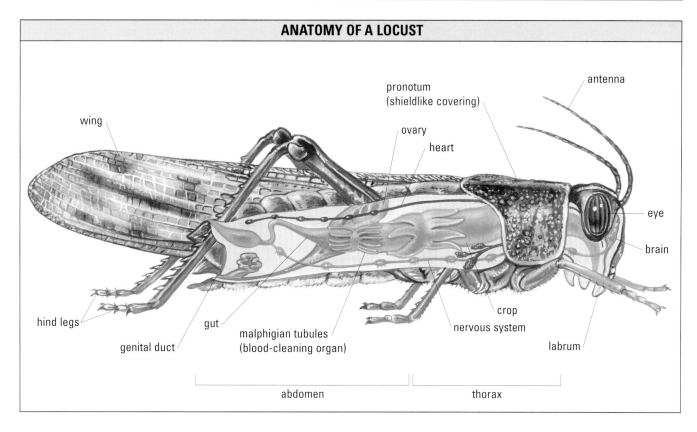

pronotum
(shieldlike covering)

antenna

ovary

heart

wing

eye

brain

crop

nervous system

hind legs

gut

labrum

genital duct

malphigian tubules
(blood-cleaning organ)

abdomen

thorax

▲ *The internal body parts of a locust. The basic body plan of orthopterans has not changed for millions of years.*

KEY FACTS

Name
Greenhouse stone cricket
(*Tachycines asynamorous*)

Food
Leaves and decaying material

Habitat
Greenhouses and basements; introduced to United States from Asia

Size
0.5 inches (13 mm)

crops over many hundreds of square miles, causing famine and great hardship for local people. The similar North American migratory locust has now been successfully controlled by humans. However, hordes of Mormon crickets threatened to wipe out the crops of farmers in Utah in the middle of the nineteenth century. The crops were saved when the swarm was eaten by flocks of hungry seagulls.

Other species of grasshoppers, such as the pallid band-winged grasshopper, have occasional population explosions, but these are considered to be more of a nuisance than an agricultural pest.

Several species of crickets are adapted to living in or around human dwellings and have been transported around the world through commerce. The Indian house cricket originally lived in Asia but is rapidly becoming established in cities throughout North America.

The greenhouse flat stone cricket is an Asian species introduced throughout parts of North America and Europe, where it now lives in warm greenhouses and basements.

Moles and mole crickets

Mole crickets are large insects that live underground, where they feed on insect larvae and the roots of plants. Like many other orthopterans, they communicate using sound. The males vibrate their wings and use the walls of the burrow to amplify the sound.

Mole crickets are streamlined so they can move through the soil, and they have a tough covering that protects their bodies from the rubbing action of the soil. Their most remarkable adaptations, however, are their forelegs. These are forward pointing and broad, with a series of sharp fingerlike spines. Mole crickets use these legs to shovel soil backward, digging in exactly the same way as a mole, which has similar front limbs.

Animals from different groups that have similar lifestyles often share physical similarities. This is called convergent evolution.

Beneficial insects

Some orthopterans are very useful to people. The European house cricket is a common pest in houses around the world, but it is also bred commercially and sold in North America as live bait and food for pets.

▶ *This is a katydid nymph. Unlike the larvae of insects such as ants, flies, and beetles, young orthopterans look like smaller versions of the adults.*

▼ *As their name suggests, mole crickets live underground. Their front legs are large, flattened, and bear a set of claws. Mole crickets use these limbs to push away soil as they dig their tunnels.*

Other orthopterans are used as biological control agents, reducing the need for insecticides to control crop pests. One species of cricket preys upon insect pests that feed on rice crops in Asia.

Edible orthopterans

Grasshoppers are often plentiful and are a good source of protein. People around the world consume katydids and grasshoppers, even those that are pests. Marauding migratory locusts in Africa are occasionally consumed, as are bush crickets. In Mexico, grasshoppers are carefully prepared with onion, garlic, and chili powder before being boiled and dried in the sun.

Endangered grasshoppers

Many species of orthopterans are threatened by habitat loss, as well as competition with introduced species. There are at least 82 species of grasshoppers and crickets around the world that are close to extinction. One U.S. species, the zayante band-winged grasshopper from California, is endangered. However, the Antioch Dunes shield-back katydid and the Central Valley grasshopper are believed to have already disappeared.

GREAT DIVING BEETLE

Among the largest of all aquatic insects, great diving beetles are fearsome predators that feed on fish and tadpoles as well as other invertebrates.

Great diving beetles are among the largest aquatic beetles. Adults can be between 1 and 1.5 inches (2.5 and 4 cm) long. They are easily recognized by their large size, yellow or reddish undersides, and by various yellow markings around the edges of the thorax (midbody) and elytra (wing cases). The elytra of some females are covered with ridges. There are 26 species of great diving beetles in North America, Europe, and northern Asia.

Adults and larvae, also known as "water tigers," are active predators. Usually they hunt and eat various kinds of aquatic insects, but some have been seen killing tadpoles, small fish, and in one case, even a snake. A beetle larva can eat several tadpoles in one day.

Great diving beetles are usually found in lakes, permanent ponds (ones that do not dry up in late summer), and slow moving areas of rivers. Both adults and larvae can be found in the same places. Adults carry an air supply under their wing cases, while the larvae use gills.

Adult beetles spend the winter under water and live for a few months in the next year. Early in the spring, they breed, and the larvae develop rapidly, taking approximately four to five weeks to reach maturity. Mature larvae leave the water and pupate in soil along the banks of the river or pond.

Adult great diving beetles are not commonly seen, except sometimes flying toward lights at night. The best way to catch them is in underwater traps that make use of fluorescent "glow sticks." Apparently, the beetles are attracted to lights under water as well as when flying. However, when captured, both adults and larvae can inflict a very painful bite if handled carelessly.

▲ *A male (right) and female (left) European great diving beetle. The hind legs are hairy to help the beetles push themselves through the water.*

SEE ALSO

- Beetle
- Carrion beetle
- Soldier beetle
- Water beetle
- Water bug

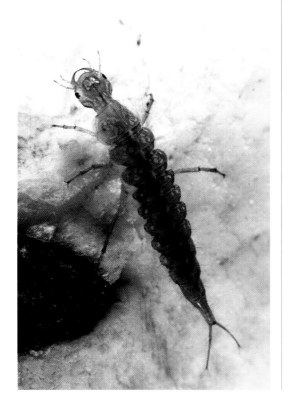

◀ *A newly hatched great diving beetle larva. The insect's mouthparts are pincerlike for catching prey.*

GROUND BEETLE

The ground beetles are a diverse family living around the world. Many species are important, as they feed on other animals that are agricultural and garden pests.

The ground beetle family contains many species. Scientists do not know exactly how many, but they estimate that there are probably between 25,000 and 40,000 different types. With so many members in the family, it can be difficult to reliably identify and classify the different species of ground beetles. To do this, entomologists (insect scientists) look at the exact structure of the adult beetle. In many cases, the structure of the larval stages is poorly known, and to identify a beetle larva it is often necessary to wait for it to turn into an adult.

In most biological groups, the number of different species that are present in any given area increases in the warmer tropical regions. This is also true for ground beetles. However, some species live as far north as the Arctic Circle. Some species can even survive when the temperature falls below freezing (32°F; 0°C) during cold winters.

▼ *A ground beetle in a forest in eastern Europe. The ridges and colored dots on its back are typical of many ground beetles.*

◄ *A searcher, or caterpillar hunter beetle devours a white line sphinx moth caterpillar.*

Beetle body form

Like all beetles, ground beetles have hardened wing cases formed from the first pair of wings. These wing cases are called elytra. The elytra of ground beetles meet together in a straight line down the center of the back. There are also many straight ridges that run parallel down the length of the wing cases. Between these ridges, there are patterns of dots and pits that are often used to identify particular species. In most species, the wing cases are either a dull or shiny black or brown. However, some species have a metallic sheen.

The wing cases of some species are joined together, and the hind wings beneath are small and useless for flying. In others, the wing cases are able to open up, allowing a fully functional pair of wings to be used for flight.

The antennae of ground beetles join on to the head between the eyes and the mouthparts and are present in various lengths and shapes that change from species to species. In one group of ground beetles, which live inside ants' nests, the antennae have a narrow base and are topped with large, flattened club-shaped tips. These "clubs" are thought to be used for distributing and detecting chemical signals. These chemicals are an important part of the beetles' interaction with their ant hosts.

The bodies of all ground beetles are elongated and slightly flattened. For example, the wing cases of the violin beetle are greatly enlarged and flattened. This Southeast Asian species also has an extremely long and thin head. The combination of these two features makes the beetle resemble a

DISTRIBUTION

VIOLIN BEETLE

KEY FACTS

Name
Violin beetle
(*Mormolyce phylloides*)

Distinctive features
Enlarged and flattened wing cases, long head, and long antennae

Behavior
Uses thin body to wedge itself under bark

Breeding
Eggs laid on suitable trees

Food
Insect larvae and snails

Size
Up to 4 inches (10 cm) long

Potato protector

The Colorado potato beetle is a very destructive pest that has spread from the western United States to Europe and Asia. As its name suggests, this beetle is a pest of potato crops in all these places.

However, *Lebia grandis,* a North American species of ground beetle, attacks Colorado potato beetles. The adults of *L. grandis* feed on the eggs laid by the pest species. The female ground beetles then lay eggs in the soil. As soon as the larvae hatch out, they head off in search of pupating potato beetle larvae. The ground beetle larvae feed on the pest pupae until they are ready to pupate too. The life cycle of the ground beetle is timed to coincide closely with that of the pest species.

SEE ALSO

- *Beetle*
- *Biological control*
- *Bombardier beetle*
- *June bug*
- *Scarab beetle*
- *Tiger beetle*

violin, hence the species' common name. The shape of this beetle helps it slide under tree bark in the forest.

Just like all other insects, ground beetles have six legs, and these are long and slender, being well adapted for running and walking in search of prey, mates, and suitable habitats. Although there are many ground beetle species that, despite the name, live in and around trees and shrubs, most species do live on the ground. Ground-dwelling species find their prey among vegetation, leaf mold, soil, and other debris.

Life on the forest floor is filled with dangers from falling objects, rough ground, and many types of predators. A toughened, flattened body and, for some species,

fused wing cases offer protection from these dangers. A flattened body helps the beetle keep its balance and slip into a hiding place easily when threatened by a predator.

Catching prey

Most ground beetles are predators and hunt by night. The group has evolved many ways of catching their food. For example, tiger beetles are fast moving, highly active beetles, with long, slender legs for running, large eyes for spotting their prey, and very large, sharply jagged mouthparts for gripping struggling prey.

A number of ground beetles feed upon the pests that can infest the home, gardens, and cultivated food crops such as vegetables and fruit. In many places, farmers leave strips of their fields uncultivated and untreated with pesticides (poisons that kill pests). These strips of land are called beetle banks, and they provide a route along which beetles and other predators can get into the nearby crops to catch pests such as slugs, aphids, and caterpillars.

A few species of ground beetles feed on carrion. Carrion is the remains of dead and decaying animals. Other species are adapted to eating plants or seeds. The majority are active predators, however, hunting prey by searching visually or by detecting the smell of their prey.

▼ *A violin beetle attacks a snail. Like other snailhunters, the mouthparts of these beetles are hook shaped.*

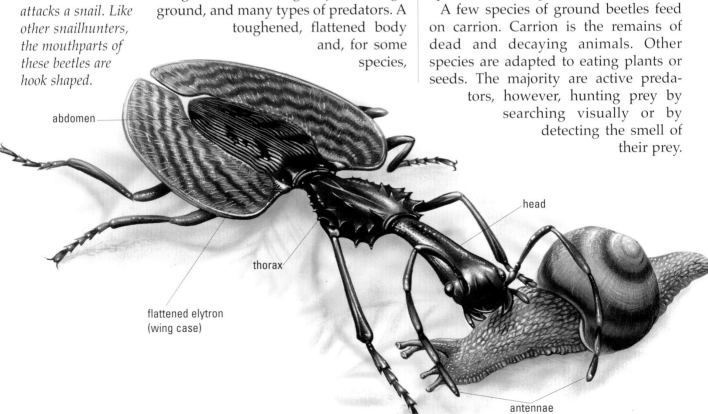

abdomen

thorax

flattened elytron (wing case)

head

antennae

Ground beetle enemies

Although they are mostly fierce predators, ground beetles have a number of natural enemies of their own. They may be parasitized by tiny nematode worms or fungi, or they may be eaten by small mammals, birds, or reptiles.

Ground beetles have evolved a number of ways to avoid predators. Many species are able to produce foul-smelling chemicals when harassed by enemies. A few species can spray a cocktail of these defensive chemicals at their attackers. Bombardier beetles are a type of ground beetle that have a very flexible abdomen from which they can squirt a mixture of hot, toxic chemicals. These beetles can direct their defensive jets accurately.

Much simpler defense techniques are employed by many ground beetles—they dig holes or run away. Some fly, but others are unable to do so quickly.

Life cycle

Female ground beetles lay their eggs singly in soil, on plants or fungi, or in leaf litter. The number of eggs laid depends greatly on the species and the habitat of the adults. It is in the egg stage that ground beetles are most at risk, because they can be invaded by fungi. The eggs that survive give rise to very active, six-legged larvae, which,

▲ *A European adult ground beetle overwinters underground. Like many species that live in colder areas, this beetle spends the long winter in an inactive state, called diapause.*

◀ *A ground beetle pupa. The legs and body parts of the adult can be seen through the toughened skin.*

much like their parents, are generally predators. The larvae are elongated and have tapered bodies, with heads bearing large mouthparts. Being larvae they lack wings and do not have compound eyes. Like the adults, the larvae are often dark brown or black.

As the larvae feed and develop, they grow in size and must shed their old, tight skin. Most species of ground beetle will molt about three times before becoming fully developed. Then, the larva's skin toughens and it becomes a nonmoving pupa. During the pupal stage, which takes place in the soil, the beetle changes into its adult form.

The development from egg to adult can take many months. The life cycle may be interrupted by winter, during which time the larvae of some species enter a state of dormancy (inactivity) called diapause. This helps the insect survive the colder and harsher conditions of the winter months, during which time food is very difficult to find.

GYPSY MOTH

Gyspy moths can be damaging pests. Although the adult moths do not feed at all, their caterpillars have been known to eat their way through forests, with devastating results.

The gypsy moth is a member of a diverse family of moths, containing between 2,500 and 3,000 species. The family also includes the tussock moths.

Form and function
Female gypsy moths are often unable to fly despite having fully formed wings. Like other members of their family, and moths in general, female gypsy moths attract males by emitting chemicals called pheromones. Males detect the females' pheromones using receptors on their featherlike antennae.

Typically for their family, gypsy moths are not brightly colored. Males have golden brown hind wings that are darker brown on the edges. The male's forewings are pale brown and are patterned with darker markings. The females have larger, rounded bodies covered with pale hairs, and both sets of wings are cream-colored with a series of brown spots around the edges. Each of the female's forewings bears characteristic, dark-brown V-shaped markings.

Both sexes have a tuft of hairs at the end of the abdomen. In the female, hairs from this tuft are used to cover the egg mass and provide protection for the eggs when they are laid. In some species that are closely related to gypsy moths, these hairs offer further protection since they can sting or irritate the skin of would-be predators.

Hairy larvae
It is not only adult gypsy moths that are hairy. The caterpillars are blue-gray and have rows of raised, hairy red and blue spots, often

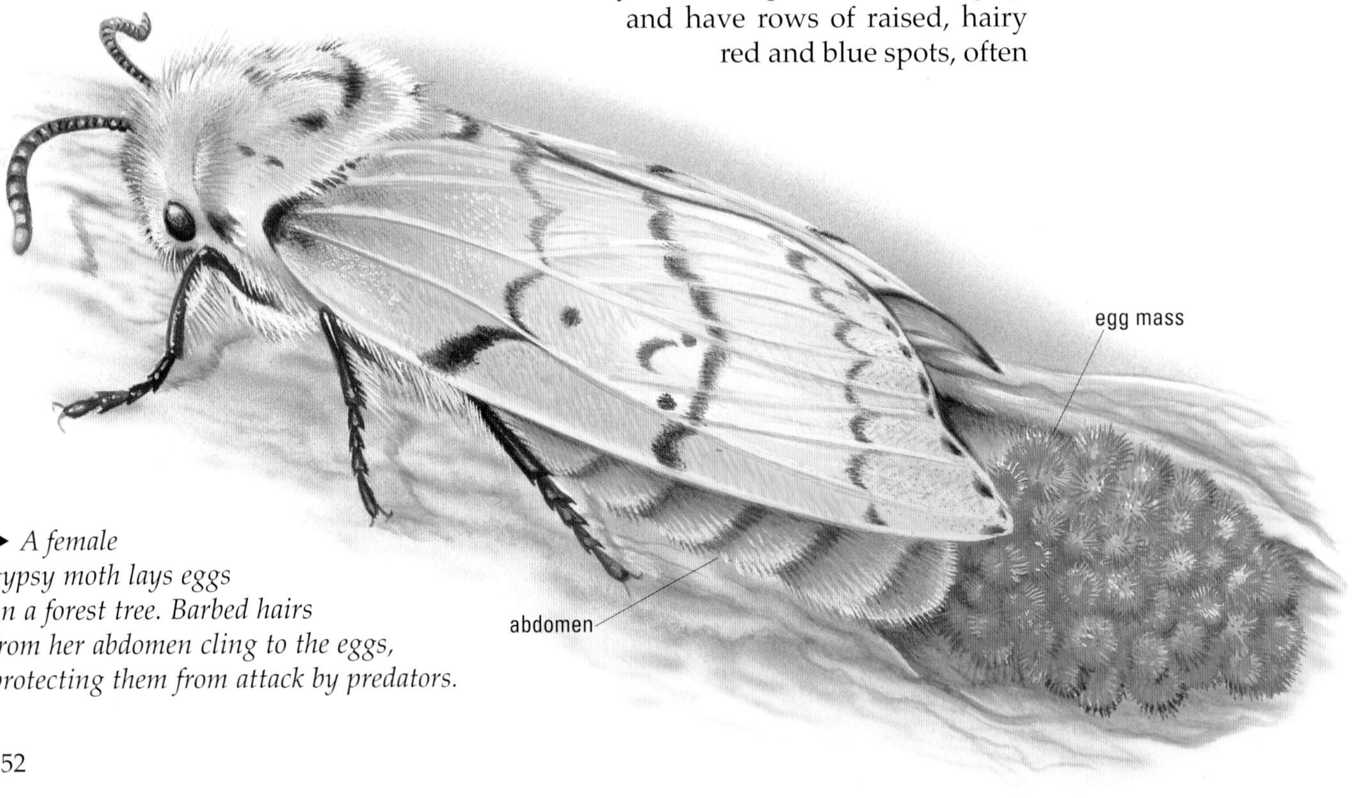

▶ A female gypsy moth lays eggs on a forest tree. Barbed hairs from her abdomen cling to the eggs, protecting them from attack by predators.

egg mass

abdomen

called warts, along their back. A larva's hairs may offer protection from attack by predators. In some cases, the hairs are barbed like a fishing hook and may even be covered in poisonous chemicals. The moth's pupal stage is formed in loose silk cocoons that may still retain the irritating larval hairs for protection.

Life cycle

Gypsy moths complete one generation each year. Females lay their eggs in batches on tree trunks, leaves, or other surfaces. The dormant eggs survive through winter, and caterpillars emerge the following spring. They develop rapidly, feeding on the newly sprouted leaves of their host tree, which is commonly an oak species.

The male larvae pass through five molts, while the females pass through six, before pupating in silk cocoons that are attached to the host tree. The adults emerge, mate, and then lay eggs before dying soon after.

Adult females do not move far after emerging from their pupa. Therefore, unusually for winged insects, it is the larvae that are responsible for the

▲ *Parts of this forest in Virginia have been almost completely stripped of leaves by gypsy moth larvae.*

◄ *An adult male gypsy moth rests on a tree trunk before flying off to find a mate. The colors of the moth's wings are similar to those of the tree bark, helping the moth hide from predators.*

spread of gypsy moths. The smallest larvae use threads of silk to catch the wind that blows them to other trees.

Becoming a pest

Unlike most adult moths, adult gypsy moths do not have any mouthparts and do not feed. However, the larvae of the gypsy moth have huge appetites that can bring them into conflict with human activities.

The caterpillars feed on most trees or shrubs but prefer to eat leaves from oak trees. When present in large enough numbers, and if environmental conditions are suitable, the gypsy moth larvae can completely strip the leaves from the trees that they occupy, often seriously damaging large areas of forest. This species of moth can be a major pest in protected woodlands and commercial plantations that grow trees for sale.

There are many examples of insect pests, such as cockroaches and Colorado potato beetles, that have been spread across the world through human activities such as trade. The gypsy moth has a similar history. The species originally lived in Europe and Asia, but in the 19th century, caterpillars were imported into the United States by people wanting to produce silk from the moth's pupal cocoons. Unfortunately, the adult moths

KEY FACTS

Name
Gypsy moth
(*Lymantria dispar*)

Distinctive features
Adult has no mouthparts; male has feathery antennae; female has hairy body

Habitat
Trees in cool temperate forests

Behavior
Larva disperses by being blown on the wind; adult female does not fly

Food
Prefers oak leaves

Lifespan
One year; eggs dormant over the winter

Size
Adult: 1.5 to 2.5 inches (4 to 6 cm)

DISTRIBUTION

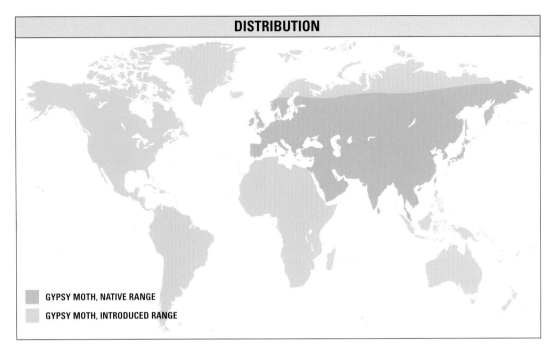

GYPSY MOTH, NATIVE RANGE

GYPSY MOTH, INTRODUCED RANGE

escaped and have now become established across much of North America. The larvae of this highly destructive insect are still being spread around the world on traded logs, wood, or other transported goods.

Pest problem solved?

The pest status of the gypsy moth changes from place to place. For example, in Europe, where the moth has many natural enemies, the moth causes much less damage to trees than it is does in North American forests.

The gypsy moth was once regarded as one of North America's most serious pests. It caused enormous amounts of damage to trees every year. However, a fungus that causes disease in the moths has recently become established in North America, and this has led to a decrease in moth numbers. Scientists do not know how this fungus reached the continent, but it seems probable that it will keep the gypsy moth population under control. Scientists believe that soon gypsy moths will no longer be a pest in the United States.

▶ *A gypsy moth caterpillar eats its way through a leaf. The larva is covered in hairs that make it difficult for predators to eat.*

SEE ALSO

- *Biological control*
- *Defense*
- *Moth and butterfly*
- *Owlet moth*
- *Pest*

GLOSSARY

abdomen: the rear body section of insects, spiders, and other arthropods

antennae (an-TEH-nee): sensitive jointed feelers on the heads of insects

anticoagulant (AN-TY-coh-AHG-yuh-luhnt): chemical released by bloodsucking insects to stop blood from clotting

arthropod (AHR-thruh-PAHD): animal with several pairs of jointed limbs and a hard outer covering (exoskeleton)

bioluminescence (BYE-oh-LOO-muh-NEH-suhnts): the production of light by an organism

book lung: a series of leaflike plates through which scorpions and some spiders breathe

cephalothorax (SEH-fuh-luh-THOR-AKS): the fused head and thorax of a spider

chelicerae (kih-LIH-suh-ree): appendages near an arachnid's mouth; those of spiders carry fangs

circadian (suhr-KAY-dee-uhn) **rhythms**: daily cycles within a living body

convergent evolution: when two unrelated organisms with similar lifestyles look or behave in similar ways

diapause (DIE-uh-POZ): a resting phase during which an insect does not grow

elytra: wing cases that protect the hind wings

exoskeleton: the hard outer covering of an arthropod; contains chitin (KEYE-tuhn)

gill: breathing organ of water-living invertebrates and some land-living species, such as pill bugs; it draws in oxygen

gravity: force that pulls objects together and holds things on the surface of Earth

halteres (HOL-TIRS): a pair of clublike organs used by flies to balance in flight

herbivore (HUR-buh-VOR): animal that only feeds on plants

host: animal that provides food and usually a place to live for a parasite

humidity: the amount of water vapor in the air

insecticide (in-SEHK-tuh-SEYED): a chemical that kills insects

invertebrate (IN-VUHR-tuh-bruht): animal without a backbone

irruption (ih-RUHP-shuhn): sudden invasion by large numbers of insects or other animals

larva (LAR-vuh): young form of insect that looks different from the adult, lives in a different habitat (type of place), and eats different foods

maggot: larva of a fly

mimicry (MIH-mih-kree): when an animal uses color, sound, or behavior to disguise itself as something else

molt: shedding of the exoskeleton by an arthropod as it grows

mutualism (MYOO-chuh-wuh-LIH-zuhm): relationship between two different species in which both parties benefit

nymph (NIHMF): young form of insect that looks similar to the adult and usually lives in a similar habitat (type of place)

ovipositor (OH-vuh-PAH-zuh-tuhr): tube on a female insect's abdomen that lays eggs

parasite: organism that feeds on another organism called a host; the host may be damaged but is not killed by the parasite

pheromone (FEH-ruh-MOHN): chemical released by an insect, often to attract mates or to direct other insects to food

phoresy (fuh-REE-see): when a small animal is carried by a larger one

pollination: transfer of pollen (male sex cells) from one flower to another, either by the wind or by animals such as insects, allowing seeds to form

predator: an animal that feeds by catching and killing other animals

pupa (PYOO-puh): stage during which a larva transforms into an adult insect

sperm: male sex cell that fuses with a female egg to create a new individual

spinneret (SPIH-nuh-REHT): silk-spinning organ found at the rear of a spider's abdomen

spiracle (SPIH-rih-kuhl): opening in the exoskeleton through which arthropods breathe

thorax: midbody section of an insect to which legs and wings are attached

trachea (TRAY-kee-uh): tube through which air travels to the cells of an insect's body

INDEX

Page numbers in **bold** refer to main articles; those in *italics* refer to picture captions.